# PRAYERS
# & DECREES
## *THAT ACTIVATE*
# ANGEL ARMIES

# PRAYERS
# & DECREES

*THAT ACTIVATE*

# ANGEL ARMIES

*Releasing God's Angels into Action*

## TIM SHEETS

DESTINY IMAGE® PUBLISHERS, INC.
P.O. Box 310, Shippensburg, PA 17257-0310
*Promoting Inspired Lives.*

This book and all other Destiny Image and Destiny Image Fiction books are available at Christian bookstores and distributors worldwide.

For more information on foreign distributors, call 717-532-3040.
Reach us on the Internet: www.destinyimage.com.

ISBN 13 TP: 978-0-7684-6313-2
ISBN 13 eBook: 978-0-7684-6314-9
ISBN 13 HC: 978-0-7684-6315-6
ISBN 13 LP: 978-0-7684-6397-2

For Worldwide Distribution, Printed in the U.S.A.
    7 8 / 26 25 24

# CONTENTS

# INTRODUCTION

God has taken me on a magnificent journey with angel armies and it continues today. The revelation He has shown me has changed my life and my ministry and I pray the same experience for you. Learning how to understand angels and the way they assist us in every aspect has been eye-opening to say the least, and especially the act of decreeing God's Word to give angels something to work with! As the ekklesia rises up and takes their place, the importance of declaring His Word has never been more important. Use this book to give insight to how to pray, how to decree, and how to release and activate angels in your daily life. I believe it will change your life as well.

# EXPONENTIAL INCREASE

**WE DECREE** greater power than has ever been seen in church history is now flowing to us and through us. Angel activity is increasing exponentially.

Caesar Creek Lake is not far from my house. I have gone there to pray and seek the Lord for years now. In the fall of 2003, I was there again at one of my favorite places way back in the woods, facing a waterfall. As I asked Holy Spirit to clarify direction for the church, an amazing download began. Holy Spirit talked to me about another Pentecost He would soon steward upon the earth. He revealed that a new move of God would soon begin, a move that He described as an "awakening surge greater than the world has ever seen." He also revealed how His angels would assist, stating very clearly, "*This time I am coming with far more of the angel armies.*" To say He had my undivided attention would be an understatement. I was not expecting that statement at all.

As I sat pondering what was being said, Holy Spirit then branded a phrase into my spirit that I have declared hundreds of times since. It was as though He carved it into my DNA. He said, "*The greatest days in church history are not in its past, they are in its future.*" The significance of that statement was enormous. Something greater than any move of God's Kingdom in history would now surge. Greater Kingdom power than has ever been seen will now flow from Christ's New Testament church. Enlightenment came that there is now an alignment of Heaven's angel army with the remnant warrior army and with what I now call the "war eagle" army from the coming generation. They will now synergize under Holy Spirit supervision to demonstrate that the Kingdom of God is present and functioning in great power.

From that very special day, Holy Spirit led me through the Scriptures, teaching me about His angel army. I was captivated by the revelation as, month after month, more was revealed. Yes, I knew angels were real, but they were not on my radar as Holy Spirit was now teaching. Awareness began to come of one of the greatest benefits to God's heirs—angel assistance. After months of research and study, the picture was now even clearer: "*The greatest days in church history are not in its past, they are in its future.*" Holy Spirit would supervise the greatest movement of the Kingdom of Heaven and it would happen in my time. I knew that this movement would move. It is meant to move. It is "move-meant," propelled by supernatural power. I knew that angel armies were behind this movement and that hell has never faced anything like it, nor have the remnant warriors. Holy Spirit is now marshaling His armies to change history.

## HOLY SPIRIT,

*Open my eyes to see what Your Spirit and Your angel armies are doing now in the earth. I choose to partner with You and agree with You that the greatest days in church history are not in its past, but in its future.*

# ANGELS AND REGIONAL BREAKTHROUGH

**WE DECREE** Heaven's army is being released in this region!

Psalm 103:19-22 (KJV) says, "*The Lord hath prepared his throne in the heavens; and his kingdom ruleth over all. Bless the Lord, ye his angels, that excel in strength, that do his commandments, hearkening unto the voice of his word. Bless ye the Lord, all ye his hosts; ye ministers of his, that do his pleasure. Bless the Lord, all his works in all places of his dominion: bless the Lord, O my soul.*"

Holy Spirit inspired King David to use incredible wording in this passage. The word *excel* is the Hebrew word *gibbor*. It means "warrior, valiant one, or champion" (Strong, H1368). But *gibbor* is the same as the Hebrew word *gebulah* or *gebul*. That is important to understand because *gebulah* means "territory, region, boundaries, landmarks, coasts, or limits" (Strong, H1367).

Angels help maintain boundaries for the Kingdom of God. They are Holy Ghost-led border patrol agents. They assist us in maintaining our regions. They are warriors valiantly fighting to open territories or guard territories. They help us set the landmarks that state, "God rules this territory." They help set the landmark that says, "This is Kingdom territory. This is God territory. God rules this geography." When an apostolate declares what God says into their regional (territorial) assignment, angels hearken and help clear the territory and establish the rule of King Jesus. They assist all His works in all places of His dominion. When we declare the dominion of King Jesus over a region, angels begin to assist in establishing it. Fellow servants begin to patrol the boundaries. They will war in the natural realm or the spirit realm.

Fellow servants will then begin to administer the covenants we have declared there in Jesus' name.

- Strength (Hebrew: *kowach*)—force, to be forceful, to be firm, or to produce. They are hearkening to produce the Word of God that's been decreed (Strong, H3581).
- Commandments (Hebrew: *dabar*)—business, cause, matter, or purpose. They do the King's business in the region (Strong, H1697).
- Pleasure (Hebrew: *ratson*)—desire, will, or inclination (Strong, H7522). They do whatever the King is inclined to do. They do whatever He wants done. They do whatever the other self, Holy Spirit, wants done.

It's easy to see that the angels' assignment and our assignment are very similar. We are also to do whatever the King is inclined to do. We are to do whatever He wants. We are to establish His reign in our territory. We are to establish His will in our region. We are to set boundaries that declare, "God reigns here. Entering Kingdom territory. Entering God territory. Entering territory where the King's covenants are maintained, guarded, and enforced by Holy Spirit, by saints here, and by the angel armies." We are to declare His dominion. We are to declare against hell's forces, "Your strategies are off-limits. You cannot enter." If we dare declare the Word of the Lord and prophesy what it says, His hosts will then mobilize. And great victory, deliverance, and miracles can come into our region—*we can shift the territory so it aligns with the Word of God!*

## KING JESUS,

*I declare that my home and region are set apart for Your glory. I welcome the angels of Heaven to establish the Kingdom of God in my hometown, state and nation. May Your reign and Lordship be established now.*

# DIVINE ASSISTANCE FOR FULFILLED DESTINY

> **WE DECREE** we were born for these times. We declare our potential is loosed and angel assisted, in Jesus' name.

An amazing benefit of the ministry of angels is how they assist the releasing of destiny. Angels help the heirs of God and joint heirs with Christ to understand their purpose and potential. This is vital to understand. Quite frankly, because of poor teaching, no teaching, or a Western mindset that has trivialized angels, millions of believers today just wander through life not understanding the real purpose for their being. We can understand, and angels are sent to help us understand.

The Scripture reveals that to see our destinies come to fullness, we all need assistance. No one achieves great significance in life without a lot of assistance. We need the assistance of the Holy Spirit. He is the number-one source for direction and guidance. Also, we need each other. Much of our destiny is interdependent. That's why we need the church and the body of Christ. Without others mentoring, instructing, resourcing, assisting, working with us, some of our purpose will never be accomplished. Also, there are aspects of our destiny that we will never see come to fullness without angel assistance.

We need to understand and embrace that God decided it be that way. God decided that we would need to be angel assisted to accomplish at least some of our purpose. In their wisdom, the Godhead provided "destiny enablers," sending angels to assist the heirs to discover and release their potential.

To see the greatest move of God in history, this must happen. I believe it's why Holy Spirit has led the church through a great season of transition. People are being shifted and connected to times that they were actually born for. It's happening everywhere and there's a sense that we are here for such a time as this. I know in many ways, I myself feel that I am now entering into times that were ordained for me before I was ever born. It's as though I have been prepared up until now for days that are about to unfold. God's remnant people, the remnant believers, are beginning to think similar types of thoughts—*I am here for the greatest harvest in all of history, I am here for now, I am here for the great outpourings of the Holy Spirit, I was made for these times.*

Acts 17:26 says that God appoints your time and your place. The reason you are here right now is because God wants you here right now. You could have been born 500 years ago or during the Persian Empire, but you were not. God ordained your time and place (geographic location). You're alive now because God wants you alive now. That means there is something in your destiny that the world needs now, especially the area in "the boundaries of your habitation." God in His infinite wisdom knows this, and with Holy Spirit assistance, angel assistance, and the body of Christ assistance He wants it released.

GOD,
*I ask for Your wisdom and insight to understand my destiny.*
*Thank You for allowing me to be alive for such a time as this.*
*I invite the assistance of the angel armies and Your assistance,*
HOLY SPIRIT, *to see greater measures of Your glory displayed on the earth and in my life.*

# HEAVENLY PARTNERSHIP

> **I DECREE** angels assigned to me the day I was born have been briefed concerning my purpose, and they are partnering with me to accomplish God's will for my life.

Before you were ever born, before there was a single day to you, God wrote down the plans and destiny He had in mind for you. Before you were ever put into your mother's womb, He recorded in His book things about your life. That's amazing to contemplate. The Godhead actually wrote down things about you.

Second Timothy 1:9 (KJV) says, *"Who hath saved us, and called us with an holy calling, not according to our works, but according to his own purpose and grace, which was given us in Christ Jesus before the world began."*

Again, before time began God established your purpose. *Purpose* is the Greek word *prothesis* and it's one of my favorite words to talk about. *Pro* means "before, to set before, to set up beforehand, or an exposition." *Thesis* means "a written report, an essay, or a composition." *Before you were born, God wrote your thesis.* He wrote your purpose and the plans He had for you. There was a day somewhere in the eternities past when the Godhead sat down and contemplated why they would allow you to be. They contemplated why you would come to the earth, why they would make you, and what would be your purpose. In their book they recorded an essay on you. In Jeremiah 29:11 (NLT) God says, *"'I know the plans I have for you,' says the Lord. 'They are plans for good and not for disaster, to give you a future and a hope.'"*

God has great plans for every one of us. Your future is bright and your destiny is good. There are no disasters planned by God for your life. The enemy may have some planned, but God and His Kingdom do not. His plans are only good and they are designed to give you a bright future filled with hope.

Consider again the text in Matthew 18:10 (KJV) where Jesus says concerning angels and little ones, children, or infants, *"Take heed that ye despise not one of these little ones; for I say unto you, That in heaven their angels do always behold the face of my Father which is in heaven."*

In light of this great benefit that Jesus Himself points out, the angels assigned to your life are most certainly briefed about your destiny. How could they assist your purpose if they don't understand it? How could they assist your destiny unless they were briefed about what your destiny is? The angels who constantly view the presence of God in Heaven are taught by the Author of your purpose what your purpose is, and they are constantly looking for a time, place, or event to loose you into that purpose. This magnificent benefit shows the love, value, and special care the Godhead provides the believers in Jesus. There are no creatures anywhere on earth except the born-again ones who have this kind of care provided. You are highly treasured with divine destiny planned for you. This is emphasized by the fact that angels were assigned to help you accomplish it the day you were born!

## HOLY SPIRIT,

*Your wisdom and goodness are beyond comprehension. I surrender afresh today to Your purposes for my life. Thank You for Your careful design and plan. I choose to partner with the angels assigned to my life to see You receive the glory You deserve.*

# THE GREAT CONNECTORS

> **WE DECREE** angels who connect us to people, places, circumstances, events, and to our purpose—be loosed in Jesus' name.

Are there destinations in life that angels help us get to? Absolutely yes. They constantly try to connect you to a time, a place, or an event that will connect you to destiny. They can preserve, deliver, rescue, lead, and guide us to divine appointments and ordained places. Angels understanding our destiny can help us arrive safely at God-scripted destinations. Have you ever been in a situation that turned out to be a great blessing or a great connection for your life and you wonder, *how did that happen?* Perhaps it was not an accident or coincidence; it was destiny and angels connecting you.

In Judges 6, we read the story of Gideon. He was threshing wheat in the bottom of the winepress for fear of the Midianite armies. Israel's harvest had been stolen from them for seven years as the Midianites raided and plundered their land, food, and flocks, and because of it the people of God were impoverished. In fear, the Israelites ran to the hillside and hid in caves. So Gideon took his wheat to the winepress one day, and while he was threshing, *"There came an angel of the Lord, and sat under an oak which was in Ophrah, that pertained unto Joash the Abiezrite: and his son Gideon threshed wheat by the winepress, to hide it from the Midianites. And the angel of the Lord appeared unto him, and said unto him, The Lord is with thee, thou mighty man of valour"* (Judges 6:11-12 KJV).

In verse 14, we read that the angel told Gideon to go in the strength he had and rescue Israel from the Midianites. Clearly the angel of the Lord knew Gideon's destiny, his *thesis*. It was God's plan for Gideon to rescue Israel—the angel certainly knew it before Gideon did. He understood Gideon's assignment when Gideon was still fearful. Although he was hiding in fear, the angel knew his potential and addressed it by calling him a mighty man of valor. Gideon, with the Spirit of God upon him, accomplished God's purpose for his life. He and 300 warriors routed the Midianite armies and stopped the plundering of Israel's harvest.

Potential means latent abilities. They are abilities inside of you that you don't know are there. There are some abilities inside of you that you have never thought about. Angels know about those potential abilities and are constantly trying to draw them out by connecting you to a time, an event, or a place that will unlock or loose your potential. Angels, who know your destiny and have been briefed on the potential God put in your thesis, go to work to bring it out of you. *You are potent with destiny that is angel assisted.*

## LORD JESUS,

*You alone know what is possible in my life. And in Your great wisdom, You have assigned angels to help me fulfill my destiny. I thank You today for the assistance of those angels and eagerly receive their help, divine connections and insight!*

# THE WRESTLE FOR A HOPE-FILLED FUTURE

> **I DECREE** I have a God-planned future filled with great hope before me.

In Genesis 32:24, Jacob wrestled with an angel all night over his destiny. Do angels wrestle with you about your destiny? Absolutely. They are tenacious about it. Jacob had been a liar, a deceiver, and a crook who connived his way through life. He stole his brother Esau's birthright by deceiving his father, Isaac, into thinking he was Esau in order to get the blessing. Because of that Esau was filled with rage. Jacob fled and stayed away from his family for twenty years, fearful that Esau would kill him at first sight. After those twenty years, we are told an angel of the Lord appeared to Jacob in a dream and gave him a message from the Lord. Genesis 31:13 (NKJV) says, *"I am the God of Bethel, where you anointed the pillar and where you made a vow to Me. Now arise, get out of this land, and return to the land of your family."*

With fear and trembling, Jacob decided to obey. He worked for months to prepare his family to make this return to his homeland, although he still feared Esau and what he might do to his family.

In 1988, God began to wrestle with me about my destiny. It was three years of wrestling over the apostolic call on my life. I went through a time when people kept telling me I was an apostle; they would prophesy that to me. It meant nothing, and in fact, I didn't want to be an apostle, I just wanted to be a pastor. So I brushed off anything apostolic. I was in that mindset for three years, but the wrestling didn't go away; in fact, it got more and more intense. I became very dissatisfied with who I was inside. I knew that there was something more the Lord wanted to draw out of me.

At that point I didn't understand that whatever you do as an apostle isn't about you, it's about Him. In myself I have no authority and I can't do anything. It's the office that carries the authority, but I didn't understand that. I was just looking at my own limitations not understanding the authority of the Kingdom given through a mantle.

After accepting this apostolic call, different angels were assigned to my life and I knew it. The angels knew my destiny. They knew it before I did. They knew it while I was wrestling about it. They knew what I could potentially be because it was in my thesis. One of them appeared to me in Indianapolis and said, "Stop wrestling and start decreeing who you are. Accept the mantle. It's not about you." It has changed the way I walk, and my destiny has gone to a different level.

The wrestling you have been going through might be the angel saying, "Stop wasting your potential and become who you're supposed to be." *You have a God-planned future filled with great hope before you.* Like Jacob, and like me, stop wrestling with it and decree it.

## Lord Jesus,

*I yield to You, knowing that You have a hope-filled future planned for me. I will stop wrestling with the plans You have for my life and surrender afresh to Your careful design. Draw out of me what You have placed inside of me.*

# NEW WAYS AND FRESH POWER

> **WE DECREE** gifts of Holy Spirit—be loosed in greater measure than ever before.

What Joel prophesied is coming with fresh wind and fire out of Heaven. God is coming to His church in new ways and with fresh power. Why? Because we have gone to the sapphire throne of grace, and we keep returning. We have encouraged everyone we know to do the same because heavenly graces have been released upon us via the mighty Holy Spirit. Grace gifts, the gifts of the Holy Spirit, will now be released on new levels with the assistance of angels—the word of wisdom, the word of knowledge, the gift of faith, the gift of workings of miracles, the gift of healing, discerning of spirits, tongues, interpretation of tongues, and prophecy. These gifts will now expand in their meaning, demonstration, and manifestation among us.

The world has never seen the gifts of the Spirit as they're about to come forth through heirs in all generations. The high priestly ministry of the Lord framed or activated by our confession is increasing in manifestation and will be demonstrated. It doesn't matter what hell tries in opposition; it doesn't matter what the government tries or atheists or terrorists or media or arts and entertainment. The Kingdom of God will be physically seen!

Dead, passive Christianity cannot change this mandate because God will find a remnant somewhere who will receive it. When He does, He will come out of the blue with a dynamic outpouring. He will set them on fire and endow them with so much power that it is going to shake the region wide open. Hell cannot stop it. Indeed, all flesh is the mission of this heavenly campaign and it will be done. The Holy Spirit, the angelic host, and the church, in partnership with the throne of Heaven, all agree with the King's command. It is immutable! It will be done! It will be done!

Bold authority is starting to rise up in the church. We are understanding we are not here to play patty cake with hell. We are here to stop it. Aligned with the King of Kings, Jesus, our job is to evict the devil and his regime from their strongholds. As sons and daughters of God, heirs of Christ, we have been delegated authority to do exactly that in Jesus' name. Angels are ready to partner with that effort. Can the church bring the enemies of our King to His feet to be His footstool? Yes! The church, assisted by Holy Spirit-supervised angel armies, will bind and twist His enemies into a footrest for Him. The New Testament church will release and experience great deliverance, freedom, healings, harvest, and prosperity. Jesus said it will be a glorious church prevailing over all the power of hell (Matthew 16:18).

## HOLY SPIRIT,

*I ask You to come in power, releasing Your gifts and presence into my life and into the earth. Send Your angels to release fresh boldness and authority into Your church. May King Jesus get His great reward in this day and hour.*

# INCREASE THE HARVEST

> **WE DECREE** harvest angels, be released now to accomplish our King's commission with us.

A major benefit of angel assistance is how they help apostles, pastoral leaders, and fivefold ministries shift their regions into divine alignment. It is time for a major shift in our nation and in the church. It's time to shift into harvest mode, seeing millions come to Jesus. I believe it is time to see a revival like Joel prophesied, with new outpourings of the Holy Spirit that will affect all flesh. One that will shift our young men and women from indifferent, listless living to a generation of purpose and destiny. They will prophesy the Word of the Lord. They will declare the principles of God's Word and move in great power and authority seeing signs, wonders, and miracles that God promised would happen. The strongest prophetic and apostolic generation in all of history is now beginning to emerge on the earth. That means there must come a shifting into prophetic revelation at levels we have not seen before. This will produce demonstrations of the "mightiness" of our God. Visible, tangible, undeniable, and notable miracles will be seen on this planet. There will be wonders in the heavens and the earth.

> *So I will restore to you the years that the swarming locust has eaten, the crawling locust, the consuming locust, and the chewing locust, My great army which I sent among you* (Joel 2:25 NKJV).

There is now emerging a remnant church that is beginning to believe for lost harvests to be restored. I don't know how many harvests we have lost in America or the world but it has to be a massive amount. God promised through the prophet, "Joel, your harvests are going to be restored. You're going to praise the Lord your God who is dealing wondrously with you. You will never be put to shame. You're going to receive new outpourings of the Holy Spirit. Your sons and your daughters are going to prophesy. I will show wonders in the heavens and in the earth beneath. And multitudes in the valley of decision are going to call on the name of the Lord your God."

God says, "*I am obligating Myself to restore your lost harvest. Trust Me. Be faithful. Say what I say. Decree My words and I will make My word good.*"

When God activates His promise, accelerating it to fullness, there is a release of angelic assistance. This has been true throughout history, and we are seeing it today. The fresh outpouring of the Holy Spirit that Joel prophesied will now release angels to help apostles and church leaders shift their regions into alignment with God's Word. These angels will assist in restoring lost harvests, the ingathering of new harvests, and times of great restitution, including lost income. These angels will help apostles release great deliverance into their regions and in breaking demon strongholds. This, of course, will increase the harvest, where millions will receive Jesus as Lord.

### JESUS,

*Thank You that we are now entering into a great Harvest, assisted by Your angel armies. Give us eyes to see and ears to hear how to partner with the angelic to see souls and more souls come into the Kingdom of God.*

# MINISTERS OF VALOR AND COURAGE

> **WE DECREE** Holy Spirit is now implementing a major shift in the Kingdom of God in our entire region and in this nation. He is now releasing the revival of King Jesus. It is the greatest ingathering of harvest the world has ever seen.

In Judges 6, the "angel" of the Lord appeared to Gideon. For seven straight years the Midianites raided the people of God and stole their harvests. They were greatly impoverished because of it, but it was time to stop the raiding and the lost harvests. It was time to shift into gathering harvests, and clearly an angel assisted that assignment. The angel was instrumental in shifting Gideon from a passive, intimidated, and desolate existence into a mighty leader of great valor who, with supernatural help, took 300 men and killed 15,000 Midianite warriors. Gideon, a remnant, and angels brought back the harvest.

This is ordained for our times as well. Angels, guided by Holy Spirit, are available to assist us in moving from passive Christianity into aggressive, culture-changing warriors who go get the harvest. Angels are busy drawing valor out of God's people.

On the day of Pentecost in Acts 2, a massive shift was taking place. Jesus sent His Other Self, the Holy Spirit, to begin a brand-new campaign on the earth. Holy Spirit and His angels shifted the church to new levels of ministry. *Everything* went to new levels— anointing, giftings, fruitfulness, and authority to govern and reign. Heaven's hosts were assisting Holy Spirit in an outpouring of power. They assisted in shifting the ministry of apostles to new regions. Holy Spirit came with angel armies to assist the apostles in transforming regions with the Gospel of Jesus Christ. History records entire regions were affected as God's power produced signs, wonders, miracles, and great healings as Holy Spirit and angels connected their activities to the apostolic campaign.

It is time for a new outpouring of the Holy Spirit and for some fresh fire to come upon the people of God. It's time for the apostles and the apostolates to transform their regions with a Gospel of power. It's time to break from confinement to great liberty. It's time for resources to be restored and multiplied. It's time to stop the raids of hell that steal our harvests. It's time to stop wandering around in the wilderness and cross over into a new region. It's time for the church to rise to a new level of power and authority that God has ordained for our times. It's time for God's people on earth to get in sync with Heaven and run with the coming generation. It's time for the church to hear fresh orders from Heaven and campaign together, releasing the anointing of King Jesus. It is time, in Jesus' name, to shatter the teeth of chewing, crawling, and consuming locusts and, under the breaker anointing of our King, arise to scatter and shatter the constraints of hell, the restraints of government, society, or anything else that gets in the way of the Kingdom of Almighty God. Under Holy Spirit supervision and angelic assistance, *it's time to shift from harvest lost to ingathering!*

### KING JESUS,

*I ask You now for a fresh outpouring of the Holy Spirit and for Your fire to come upon Your people once again. Restore what the enemy has tried to take from the church. Today, may Your angels minister great boldness and valor in and through Your people.*

# BATTLE FOR THE THRONE

> **WE DECREE** Holy Spirit empowerment, strategies, and Angel Armies will assist the New Testament church to bind hell's tactics and loose the Gospel of the Kingdom.

Jesus says, *"My church, consisting of My heirs, are to rule and reign with Me in their region."* Authority has been given to Christ's heirs, the born-again ones, to make rulings on the earth for or against something. "Be verbal," the King says. We have been given authority in Jesus' name to overrule things on the earth. We can overrule hell's government. We can even overrule natural government by asking for divine assistance. We can ask for angel armies to be loosed to back up the rulings that we make.

Jesus says, *"Whatsoever thou shalt bind on earth shall be bound in heaven: and whatsoever thou shalt loose on earth shall be loosed in heaven"* (Matthew 16:19 KJV). The word *bind* and the word *loose* are both courtroom terms—they are legal rulings. You can have a binding contract or you could go to court and have a contract dissolved or loosed.

The Greek text has fascinated me for years. Jesus literally says, in Matthew 16:18-19, when you put all of the Greek tenses to it: "Whatever you at any time encounter of hell's council (hell's leadership/government), that I am determined my *ekklesia* will prevail against, you will then face a decision as to whether or not you will bind it. What transpires is conditional upon your response. If you do purposely and consciously involve yourself in binding the issue on earth, you will find at that future moment when you do, it is already bound in Heaven."

*Jesus says that what is bound or loosed is conditional upon the church's response.* "If it's bound by My people in My name, or loosed on earth by My people in My name, Heaven will back it up. My throne will rule in your favor and sufficient force will be released to enforce it. My angel armies will be sent to assist."

The battle is for the throne of the region. If you overthrow hell's kingdom in Jesus' name by binding spirit princes and then occupying the seat of power as a vigilant ruling body under Christ's authority, then it's much easier to get rulings accomplished upon the earth because you removed hell's power that was trying to come against it. The battle is won in the spirit before you ever see it in the earth. Jesus said, "If My church will battle for the throne of their region and will bind hell's kingdom, hell's kingdom will not prevail because I, Lord Sabaoth, will release angel armies to enforce their rulings."

We are to bind what Heaven wants bound and loose what Heaven wants loosed by aligning ourselves with the Word of God. Clearly, Christ Jesus expects His ekklesia to declare or make rulings in His name. It is to decide what is proper or improper for a region. It is to decide what is unlawful in a region. It is to decide and declare the way culture ought to be. It is important to remind ourselves that Jesus said this, not a disciple, not some other character in the Bible. The King Himself said this. The church is to decree God's Word in a region.

## HOLY SPIRIT,

*I understand the church has responsibility to decree Your powerful Word. Today, I decree that I will speak Your Word in my life and in my region, releasing angelic assistance and seeing supernatural breakthrough. I declare that Your church will respond and our region will be won for the Kingdom of Heaven.*

# ANGELS AND THE THIRD GREAT AWAKENING

> **WE DECREE** we are here to establish the rule of God's Word, His statutes, His covenants, His laws, and His principles, and King Jesus is releasing Angel Armies to help us do it.

It is vital we speak the truth without compromise, remembering Psalm 103:20—angel armies hearken to God's Word that we decree. When angels hear us declare what God says, they get involved in bringing it to pass. They assist us based on the Word of God. If we want angel armies fighting alongside of us, which we absolutely need if we are going to change nations, then we must declare what God says. If we want the Holy Spirit releasing power from Heaven, we have got to agree with the Word of God and speak it boldly. There can be no cowardly silence in the pulpit or the pew.

In the early 1800s, what most today think were the "good ole days" in our nation, we find a different reality. Our government then was corrupt and divided. Slave issues and poverty were stifling our people. The education system was inept. Society was about as bad as it gets. We actually had politicians shooting one another in duels. The church at the time was in passive mode, just like now. The chief justice of the Supreme Court at the time was John Marshall, and he wrote a letter to then President James Madison regarding the condition of the church. He wrote, "The church is too far gone to ever be redeemed." Obviously that proved not to be true. It wasn't true then and it's not true now. John Marshall's surmising did not happen because the people of God began to pray. Cottage prayer meetings began to spread from coast to coast.

Midweek prayer meetings began to be everywhere all over the United States. Even lunch hour prayer meetings started. Passionate preaching began to flame from the pulpits and great evangelists came on the scene and began to preach fiery messages of repentance. God's Word was welcomed in the pulpits and proclaimed with holy boldness, and the church was awakened from slumber by the Holy Spirit. It was simply called the Second Great Awakening, and it's going to happen again. There's going to be a third one!

The third and greatest awakening has now begun, and angels from their spheres are going to assist it. It doesn't matter how many chariots the enemy has, their size, or how many demon armies are behind them. It doesn't matter what their philosophies are or how much media they have behind them. They are not a match for the Kingdom of Almighty God.

The Lord says, "I will pour out My Spirit upon all flesh," which can only mean that it's going to happen. The remnant church will declare what God says, and angels orbiting are going to hear and they are going to begin fighting alongside of us from their spheres. They are going to fight hell with the people of God and we are going to win. Millions and millions are going to be saved and confess Jesus as Lord. Our King Jesus is going to have His harvest, and hell is not going to stop it.

## LORD JESUS,

*Give Your remnant church fresh fire for our day and age. And as we speak Your words with renewed boldness, may Your angels partner with us to see victory won for the Kingdom of God. Pour out Your Spirit! We need a fresh touch from You.*

# UGLY TO LOVELY

> **WE DECREE** miraculous outcomes are in season!
> Angels are circling to make ugly situations turn to lovely.

Psalm 34:7 (KJV) says, *"The Angel of the Lord encampeth round about them that fear him, and delivereth them."* The Living Bible says, *"For the Angel of the Lord guards and rescues all who reverence him."*

*Encampeth* is the Hebrew word *chanah* and it means "to pitch a tent, to abide, to set a siege, or to watch" (Strong, H2583). *Chanah* is closely compared to the Hebrew word *chanan,* which makes it even more meaningful. *Chanan* means "to favor, have mercy, show mercy, and it sometimes means to make lovely" (Strong, H2604).

*Round about* is the Hebrew word *cebiybah* meaning "to circle, to revolve around, or to border" (Strong, H5439). Angels, representing Christ Jesus, are commissioned to watchfully circle us and protect our borders. They hover over our lives similar to how they hovered over the 120 in the upper room in Acts 2:3. Guarding us, protecting us from demon intrusion, circling us to surround with God's grace. They hover over the heirs of Christ to minister mercy and show kindness. Angels are commissioned by the Godhead to watch over us and make things lovely.

Most certainly, not everything that happens to us is lovely. You don't have to make things lovely if they are already lovely. Sometimes you need "turn-a-rounders" who make the ugly lovely. Our planet is corrupted by sin. Our culture is polluted by sin. However, we have commissioned real beings who stick with the assignment of making things lovely. Angels surround us with supernatural favor to turn things around.

We are in a great season in the body of Christ. This is a season for dramatic turnaround in the church, our individual lives, our finances, and, I believe, in this nation. This doesn't mean that everything that happens to us is going to be lovely, but it does mean that everything can be turned that way. Angels are extensions of the Holy Spirit to our lives individually and to our corporate life as a church. They are helpers on assignment to guard the saints.

Again, the ugly can be turned around. Miraculous outcomes are in season!

One of the greatest examples of the ugly being turned to lovely occurred on the Day of Pentecost (Acts 2). On that day Jesus sat down at the right hand of Father God in Heaven. It was coronation day—the day Jesus was anointed as King of Kings and Lord of Lords. Father poured the horn of holy anointing oil over Jesus' head, which flowed down and dripped onto His body which was seated in the upper room (this is pictured in Psalm 133). What an amazing outpouring! The same anointing on the Head is now on the Body. Amazingly, just fifty days prior Jesus had been crucified. Without question that event was ugly. The cross was an ugly mess. Could that ever be turned around? The heirs know the answer. It was not possible for death to hold Him. Fifty days later, Holy Spirit and His army came into an upper room where 120 disheartened disciples gathered and turned the ugly to lovely!

## HOLY SPIRIT,

*Thank You that in Your presence all things are possible. Thank You that Your angels are being loosed now to bring great turnarounds in my life and in the lives of those around me. Jesus' sacrifice has the final word and the ugly is turning to lovely now in His precious name!*

# THE DIVINE TURNAROUND

> **WE DECREE,** in Jesus' name, angels are loosed to take hold of bad circumstances and events on life's journey and turn them around for our good.

*Likewise the Spirit also helpeth our infirmities: for we know not what we should pray for as we ought: but the Spirit itself maketh intercession for us with groanings which cannot be uttered. ...And we know that all things work together for good to them that love God, to them who are the called according to his purpose* (Romans 8:26, 28 KJV).

The word *helpeth* is the Greek word *sunantilambanomai*. It's a phrase that means "to take hold together with" (Strong, G4878). The Holy Spirit and His angels *take hold together with*. Angels circle the saints to get hold of things with them. I know they have gotten hold of things in my own life. Angels are assigned to grab on to ugly situations that we are grappling with and turn them around for good. It's a part of their job description. They are hovering over believers today, attending their lives, waiting for them to declare their freedom and exercise their authority. They are waiting for them to decree what God says in His Word. Angels watch and listen so they can turn things around according to our decrees.

A remnant is beginning to understand that we have an angel army assisting us. Mighty angels with strength, skill, wisdom, and power are available to partner with us in releasing the Kingdom of Almighty God on the earth in greater measure than ever before. The world has never seen anything like it. Hell has never experienced anything like it.

In many ways the church has never done anything like it before. New things are on the horizon, things that will startle the world. Christ's Kingdom is going to flow in authority and power with signs, wonders, and miracles exponentially seen!

Even though we face difficult times and situations that turn ugly, *sunantilambanomai*, Holy Spirit, and our angel network can get hold of it together with us and turn the ugly to lovely. Understanding this sets our faith and anchors our souls. While the angels may not be able to bring things full circle to be the same as they were (some things are never going to be the same as they were because of relationship changes, covenant breaking, or even death), and while it may be different than what you wanted or expected, angels assisting Holy Spirit can turn things around for you. *You are never sentenced to a problem if you are an heir. It is a season—not a sentence!* Trust God, declare what He says, and angels will start turning things around!

We are told in Daniel that lucifer and his angels seek to change times, laws, or seasons. If bad angels do that, how much more can the good angels, anointed by God, change your season? Seasons change. Seasons can come to an end and angels are here to help change and shift the season. I can testify that angels have changed the season many times for me. It's a part of their job description.

## HOLY SPIRIT,

*I believe that angels are hovering over me now waiting to be loosed on my behalf. Thank You for their help and assistance to bring Your goodness into my life, changing my seasons and bringing great breakthrough. I ask now for Your great hope to fill me afresh as my season is shifting in Jesus' name!*

# Evangelism Mode

> **WE DECREE** angels are loosed to lead us
> to unbelievers who are receptive to Jesus.

Another job angels have been given is to lead sinners to those who will witness Christ to them. In Acts 10, we find a fascinating chapter on angels and evangelism. It was time for the apostles to shift their vision to include everyone on the earth. Christ had given the command for the Gospel to be preached to Gentiles. A new move of the Kingdom was called for, so Holy Spirit and His angels went to work.

An angel was sent to Cornelius, the captain of an Italian band of soldiers, who told him, "Send men to Joppa. Find a man named Simon Peter. Ask him to come visit you and he will describe how you and your household can be saved." Cornelius didn't know Peter, but he obeyed what the angel said.

Meanwhile, the Holy Spirit was dealing with the apostle Peter, saying, "Peter, three men are seeking you. They are Gentiles, but I want you to go with them and don't doubt anything."

At first, Peter argued about it saying, "We can't do that; that's against the law, and that's not how we do things." But the Holy Spirit said, "It's how we do them now. We are changing things. It's a new day. Christ's sacrifice on Calvary is for the Gentiles also." This, without a doubt, was world-changing revelation being given to the apostle Peter. Holy Spirit said, "It is time for a new campaign of the church on earth. It's time to shift into a different mode. It's time for a new movement. It's time for My remnant to move and embrace a Gentile harvest for King Jesus." That changed everything. It changed the world and history. Holy Spirit supervised it, using angels to make this evangelism shift. Holy Spirit talked to the apostles and sent an angel to talk to Cornelius.

Cornelius and his household were the first Gentiles to ever receive and embrace salvation.

When we pray for the lost (an unsaved friend or loved one), when we declare words of freedom over their lives for salvation, angels can assist and begin to deal with them behind the scenes. Peter didn't know an angel was dealing with Cornelius. They were removing the spiritual blinders from a Gentile household. Angels partner with the saints to extend the Gospel message. It's one of the greatest benefits we have. Holy Spirit convicts of sin and the angels lead the lost to those who will witness to them. We need to be willing to pray, "Holy Spirit, I submit to Your ways. Release the angels to connect me to those who need me to witness the power of the Gospel to them."

The New Testament church in our times must shift into evangelism mode as never before. The angels are present to assist us. They are here to connect us to those who are open to the Gospel. The "watching" angels see what we can't see. They see opportunities! We must embrace this supernatural partnership, asking Holy Spirit to release it in full measure. Angels, evangelists, and evangelism must be loosed on the earth by the prayers and decrees of the church. The time is now!

## LORD JESUS,

*Because of Your sacrifice and the powerful presence of the Holy Spirit, today I am filled with fresh hope and expectation for those I love to say "yes" to relationship with You. I ask You, Lord, to release in full measure angels of evangelism to minister to those who do not yet know You as Savior. I decree a great harvest is coming now in Jesus' name!*

# THE POWER OF INTERCESSION

> **WE DECREE** angels who organize around
> the prayers of the saints and help bring
> them to pass are working now in our lives.

One way that God answers the prayers of His people is through angels. In Daniel 9:21-13 and 10:12-13, the angel Gabriel was sent with an answer to Daniel's prayers. God assigns angels to bring prayers to pass in the lives of heirs. What an incredible benefit. I personally think that is why prayer is fought so much in our churches today. Prayer activates angels more than any other time. Angels attend the prayer time because they are going to get assignments they can begin to work on.

Daniel was fasting and praying for 21 days in Daniel 9 and 10. He needed an answer from God. On the first day, God sent the answer through Gabriel. But we are told that the spirit prince of Persia, a demon prince, began to withstand the answer and fight it in the heavens.

God sends an answer, but somewhere in the astrological heavens the spirit prince over Persia starts to fight Gabriel to stop the answer from getting through. The warfare was so intense it lasted for 21 days. Daniel, with persistent faith, kept interceding. On the 21st day, God commissioned the angel Michael, sometimes referred to as the Prince of Israel, to go down and break up the demon resistance. Michael went with his angels and prevailed against the Prince of Persia's forces, allowing the answer to get through to Daniel. The answer was available the first day, but spiritual warfare and intercession prayer took place for 21 days.

In Acts 12:7-10, the apostle Peter was in prison because of his stand for Christ, but prayer was made by the saints without ceasing for his release. The church held a prayer meeting at John Mark's mother's house. Evidently the prayer and intercession for Peter's deliverance went well into the night. Amazingly, as they were praying for his release, an angel was sent to the jail. The angel released Peter from the shackles, opened the prison door, led him out into the city, opened the gates of the city for him, and brought him to where the prayer meeting was taking place. An angel became an answer to the church's prayer; they cried out for Peter's deliverance and angels were loosed to bring it to pass.

Heaven's angel armies are released into the affairs of men as a result of our crying out to God. Our prayer rooms may not have many in them—only a remnant—but angels fill that room. They are attending to receive assignments. They are there to hear decrees they can assist. They are attending to bring prayers up before God and minister answers. They are there to minister protection and deliverance. Prayer time releases more angel activity than any other time.

### GOD,

*Thank You for the amazing partnership that exists between Heaven and Your church. Thank You that as I pray and decree Your Word, angels are being released to see those prayers come to pass. Fill me with a renewed fervor to pray and intercede and, in turn, see angels loosed into every situation.*

# ANGELIC ASSISTANCE WITH KINGDOM ALIGNMENT

> **WE DECREE** angels who go before us to open doors—be loosed in Jesus' name.

Angels go before us to open doors for us. In Exodus 23:20 (KJV), God told Moses and his people just as they are about to leave the land of Egypt and go to their promised land, *"Behold, I send an Angel before thee, to keep thee in the way, and to bring thee into the place which I have prepared."*

Exodus 23:23 (KJV) says, *"For mine Angel shall go before thee, and bring thee in unto the Amorites, and the Hittites, and the Perizzites, and the Canaanites, the Hivites, and the Jebusites: and I will cut them off."* The captain of angel armies, Lord Sabaoth depicted here, has the angels go before us to lead us to a place that is prepared for us, cutting off the strategies of our enemies.

*Prepared* is the Hebrew word *kuwn* used 25 times in the Old Testament to refer to a dynasty. It means "to set in order, made ready, or a firm, established, fixed, and steadfast place of existence" (Strong, H3559). A dynasty references a king and his family ruling over a region, territory, or nation. God sends angels to bring us to a prepared place, an ordained place that He wants us to rule. Why? So He can establish His dynasty there.

The dynasty of the Kingdom of God that we extend in Jesus' name is prepared for advancement by angels. Angels help things come into alignment so the Kingdom can be established locally, regionally, and worldwide. Without angels, we cannot do all that the Kingdom of God needs to do in our territory. We are here to rule and reign in Christ's name. We are here to extend the jurisdiction of our God. Most certainly we have authority to do that through prayers and decrees in Christ's name that align with God's Word. If the people of God arise and boldly declare God's Word into their regions, angels will go before them to open up the opportunities as well as cut off the adversaries against it. Angels are sent to assist the church (*ekklesia*) in extending God's Kingdom throughout the earth.

The prepared place that's talked about in Exodus 23:23 was occupied by enemies. Our prepared place is also occupied. Enemies occupy the territories all around us. Every time we try to do something there are enemies of the Kingdom of God who try to resist it and stop us from going forward. The promise is that God will send His angels before us to cut them off. We are here to declare God's dynasty and to represent the rule of Jesus Christ! We have received a steadfast place of existence where we can represent our King, and angels are going before us to open doors of opportunity to us so that we can establish the Kingdom of God. To me, this is simply New Testament Christianity.

## LORD JESUS,

*Thank You that all things are possible with You. Thank You that Your angels go before me to prepare the way, cutting off every assignment of the enemy and opening up doors of opportunity for me to step into. As I move forward, may Your angels prepare the way for Your Kingdom to be established.*

# ACTIVATING THE ANGELIC

> **WE DECREE** agreement with You, Lord. We agree with Your words. We agree with Your will.

How do you mobilize angelic armies? With words of faith that decree what God says. *Words of faith activate angels; unbelief stifles angels.* Angels are watching and listening. Daniel said they are the "watchers." They hear what we say. Angels want to assist the high priestly ministry of Jesus and His Holy Spirit in our lives, but they sometimes have to simply fold their wings and look on because unbelief has stopped their assignment. I wonder how many times we have prayed and confessed God's Word and the angels activate to bring it to real manifestation in our lives and then, for whatever reason, we faint. We begin to doubt and disagree with the Word of God with our own words and conversations. And because of what we say the angels have to lay the assignment down undone. I wonder if there aren't some Christians who give their angels whiplash because they change so much. They "loose" their angels by declaring what God promises and then a few minutes later they say, "Oh, nothing is going to happen. This won't work. I doubt anything's going to change." Their fears produce words that cancel angelic assistance.

We miss awesome Kingdom benefits when we don't speak the Word of God. We certainly miss out on angels assisting God's Word to come to pass. While we have not been given authority to command angels to do whatever we want them to do (we have to have Scripture and biblical principle behind it), they are listening. Words we speak in agreement with God's Word, which we do not negate, activate angels to begin to amass the goodwill and concrete benefits of God in our lives. Promises can materialize when we stand in faith.

Holy Spirit emphasized to me years ago a simple phrase: *Idle words, idle promises. Idle words, idle angels.*

That is a powerful and yet sobering statement. *Idle* is the Greek word *argos* meaning "inactive, unemployed, useless, barren, non- working, unprofitable" (Strong, G692). Jesus said we will answer for all of our useless negative words. Idle words cause promises and angels to be nonworking in our lives. We must learn to put our angels to work with our words. We must loose them by declaring God's Word and not backing down. Bold declarations of faith deploy angels who become engaged on our behalf. Words of faith activate them to make God's promises concrete realities.

Use your authority and words of faith. Angels are waiting for you to release your authority. They are listening. Don't idle the angels with idle words. Speak words of faith at the mountain in your way, and angels will begin to cause the promise of God to begin to materialize in your life. Angels are waiting, hovering, circling, and listening for you to speak God's Word.

Are there promises, principles, or benefits you have been requesting that have not materialized in your life? If so, take heed to the words of Jesus. You have what you say. Speak words of blessing over your life and mobilize angels.

### LORD,

*Today I declare with zeal that I agree wholeheartedly with Your Word. What You say is life and peace. Therefore, I speak into every area of my life that Your Word is the greatest truth. I agree with You, Lord. I agree with You, Holy Spirit. I ask for Your angels to be mobilized now.*

# THE BLESSING OF COVENANT

> **WE DECREE** angels who watch our offerings and minister covenant rights to Christ's heirs—be loosed in Jesus' name.

The Godhead and the holy angels do not stop watching during times when tithes and offerings are received. God and His angels continue to watch in order to see if covenant is going to be honored by the heirs. If it is, angels are loosed to connect blessings to homes and vocations. They are loosed to make us sticky with favor. If covenant is not honored, angels are simply not mobilized to assist. It's as though their hands are tied. We must obey the Word of God if we want angels to connect us to biblical prosperity. They are covenant watchers circling us to administer God's good pleasure in our lives.

Jesus says in Matthew 6:4 that God will return your generosity openly. "Do not give your offerings before men to be seen of men. That way the Father who sees in secret will reward you openly." *Reward* is the Greek word *apodidomi,* which means "to give back more, to sell, to repay, or restore" (Strong, G591). The God who sees gives back more than is given. He will loose restoration to heirs who honor His Word. And He often uses His angels to assist in accomplishing this awesome benefit. They can connect you to people, places, or things that prosper you with much more than you gave.

Although some may wish that the Kingdom of Heaven closed its eyes during offerings, Scripture teaches us the opposite. They watch, not to bring condemnation or harsh judgment, but rather to have grounds upon which to bless us. Angels are not attempting to catch those walking in disobedience. That is not their assignment. They are looking to honor the covenant and identify those upon whom they can loose covenant blessings. This brings revelation to Acts 20:35, *"Remember the words of the Lord Jesus, how he said, It is more blessed to give than to receive."* How is that possible? Because the value of the reward is greater than the value of the gift.

After forty-three years of ministry, I've found that the number-one reason people do not give tithes or offerings to the Lord is they don't believe what Jesus has promised. On what do I base this? It is the only logical conclusion at which one can arrive. If you are going to get more in return and God has guaranteed it, then why would you refrain from giving?

The Living Bible says, *"It is possible to give away and become richer! It is also possible to hold on too tightly and lose everything. Yes, the liberal man shall be made rich! By watering others, he waters himself."*

The Bible clearly teaches that when we sow, we also reap. There's no ambiguity in this promise whatsoever. For if we give, it is guaranteed we shall receive. When we release what is in our hands, God releases what is in His hands.

### JESUS,

*You are the most Generous One. I pray for that same spirit of generosity to well up in me now, bringing grace into my life to honor my covenant with You. In doing so, may my giving reflect the fact that I believe Your Word and Your promises. I invite Your loving gaze into this area of my life. I want to be a joyful giver!*

# OFFERINGS AND OPEN HEAVENS

> **WE DECREE** the tithe brought to God's house causes Jehovah Jireh (our Provider) to open the heavens over our lives and families.

Offerings and the release of great blessings by angels are mentioned throughout the Scriptures. In Judges 6, the Angel of the Lord called Gideon, a mighty man of valor, to step out of his comfort zone and into a place of battle. The Midianites came every year and stole Israel's harvest, leaving the entire nation impoverished.

The Angel of the Lord appeared to Gideon and said, "You are a mighty man of valor. I want you to stop the raiding of the harvest against Israel." Out of obedience, Gideon prepared an offering and told the angel to stay there while he went to give his offering to the Lord, and the angel did exactly that. A few hours later, Gideon brought back a young, cooked goat and some bread. As he placed his offering before the Lord, the angel appeared and said, "Pour the broth over it," so Gideon did as he was instructed. When he finished, the Angel of the Lord touched the offering with his staff and fire shot out and consumed it. Then the angel disappeared.

Notice, Gideon gave an offering. I do not know what a goat cost in those days, but it cost something. There was a value to that goat. I don't know what bread cost in those days, but it cost him something—especially in a time of famine. But I do know, when he gave an offering a great breakthrough occurred. Seven years of lost harvest was restored and great victory was obtained. *Harvest*, by definition, means "success, prosperity, or abundance." First an offering was given, then success was loosed. First an offering was given, then prosperity was loosed. First an offering was given, then harvest was restored.

Malachi 3 tells us that an open Heaven occurs when we bring tithes and offerings to our God. That is extremely significant where angels are concerned as it points us toward angelic blessings and prosperity. The pathways of Heaven are opened for angels to begin to work and ascend and descend on us with great blessings.

> *"Should people cheat God? Yet you have cheated me! But you ask, 'What do you mean? When did we ever cheat you?' You have cheated me of the tithes and offerings due to me. You are under a curse, for your whole nation has been cheating me. Bring all the tithes into the storehouse so there will be enough food [provision] in my Temple. If you do," says the Lord of heaven's armies, "I will open the windows of heaven for you. I will pour out a blessing so great you won't have enough room to take it in! Try it! Put me to the test!"* (Malachi 3:8-10 NLT)

An open Heaven occurs when you bring tithes and offerings that are due Him.

Genesis 28 tells us when there is an open Heaven, angels ascend and descend. We can conclude that when we bring tithes to the storehouse, we open gates of Heaven so that angels can ascend and descend upon our lives, connecting us as heirs with rightful covenant blessings.

## GOD,

*You are Jehovah Jireh. You are my Provider. In light of Who You are, I choose to give generously and extravagantly knowing that as I give You will open the heavens over my life. May Your angels be released, and breakthrough come as I choose the way of generosity.*

# ANGELS AND THE DECREED WORD OF GOD

> **WE DECREE** angels are listening for prayers
> we pray in alignment with God's will. They are
> orbiting to hearken to God's Word that we decree.

We must align ourselves with God's Word, saying what He says. We need to believe His Word is right and declare it. Job 6:25 says that right words are forcible. The Hebrew word for *forcible* is *marats* meaning "powerful or constructive" (Strong, H4834). Declaring God's Word constructs good things to come to us. Faith decrees, based on God's Word, mobilize angels to help us build successful lives.

Of course, evil decrees of unbelief do the opposite. They mobilize demons to tear down or disrupt. Negative attitudes and statements are not simply harmless musings of a pessimist. They activate demons. We must realize the importance of our words and confess our faith based upon God's Word. If we will, angel armies will mobilize to cause God's promises to intersect with our paths.

In Matthew 12:37, Jesus commented that by your words you are "justified" and by your words you are "condemned." In Mark 11:23, He said you will get what you speak. When we say what God says, according to Psalm 103:20, angels harken to obey. Angels harken to the word of the Lord that we proclaim, but when we speak words contrary to His Word—when we speak unbelief, when we are negative, when we disagree with what God says—angels can be provoked. When the Hebrew word *marats* (forcible) is used in a negative way, it means "to irritate." Using negative words irritates your life. They irritate your destiny. Right words construct destiny and mobilize angels.

Proverbs 18:21 (NKJV) says, *"Death and life are in the power of the tongue."* We can speak our doubts or our faith. We can say what God says or what the world says. We can speak our fear or our confidence in God. Either way, there are consequences; one is good, the other bad. One looses angels and the other permits demons to operate. There are some who wonder why they see more demon activity in the church than angel activity. Perhaps it's because they activate more demons with their words than they do angels. I wonder if this isn't true in many churches. They expect demons to work against them. They expect demons to attack. And, of course, we should be alert to this and bind it in Jesus' name. *But we should expect more angel activity than demon activity.* There are more good angels than demons. It's time to loose them with words of faith aligned with God's Word. *Release angels; don't provoke them.*

It is better to say nothing than to speak unbelief and provoke angels assigned to bring about God's promises in your life. It is better to say nothing than to complain and be negative.

*We must get a revelation of how important our actions and our words are where angels and the promises of God are concerned.*

## JESUS,

*Today I choose to speak Your Word, knowing with certainty that Your words bring great breakthrough and grace. As I speak Your Word and partner with Your promises, I ask for Your angels to draw near. May Your words in my mouth loose angels into their assignments and may my belief spur them onwards as Your Kingdom is being established on the earth.*

# PARTNERING WITH ANGEL ARMIES

> **WE DECREE** the troops of Heaven, the Angel Armies, are loosed to fight alongside of us!

Angels are a divine warrior force behind the heirs of salvation, but they are not passive, naïve, unthinking beings who minister regardless of what we do. We cannot live any way we want to and have God's Kingdom behind us. We cannot live undisciplined, uncommitted lives and have the assistance of angelic hosts. We must understand that we are destined to live the life we speak. Angels know it; demons know it; but many people today do not understand it.

Our actions and our words can "ground" our Heir Force. God would not have warned us not to provoke them if it were not greatly important. Everything He says is for a reason.

It is time for a new generation of saints, new in attitude and lifestyle. It is time for a divine shift into true Christianity with the decision made to quit playing as if we are *going* to do it and for us to simply *do it*. It is time to quit pretending. It is time to conduct ourselves as believers who release the Heir Force and loose the Kingdom. It is time for the faith-decreeing church to arise. It is time to align our words boldly and unashamedly with God's Word. It is time to decree God's will on earth, done in Jesus' name. We need to empower the angel network and the Kingdom of Heaven by decreeing words of faith.

Jesus is the King of Hope. He is all powerful. We should be declaring this: that God is the same yesterday, today, and forever. Miracles are for today. The church is getting stronger and more relevant. It is prosperous. Its influence is growing. We need to decree that people are hungry for God. They want to know Him. We need to decree that the Creator is never outdated. This world's systems and all its technologies are made for now, made for us to preach Jesus as never before. What opportunities are before us! There has never been more darkness, so our light will shine brighter! The coming generation is hungry for God, and they are coming to Jesus by the millions because He has what they truly desire. They will prophesy. They will see signs, wonders, and miracles. They will move in God's power. Harvest is coming to this nation by the millions! Success is inevitable because no weapon formed against us can prosper, and if God be for us who can successfully be against us?

Our great God has promised, "I will be an enemy to your enemy and an adversary to your adversary. I'll be on your side. My angels will go before you and lead you into My promises. Live in such a way that you construct an atmosphere for My Kingdom advancement. *Do not provoke My angels. Do not ground them. Launch them! Release them with words of faith!*"

## HOLY SPIRIT,

*Thank You that You are working on our behalf. I ask for a spirit of boldness to fall afresh upon Your church, launching us into places of great faith so that You may be glorified on the earth. May Your Bride be filled with new fire to partner with Your angel network. Loose Your angel armies now in Jesus' Mighty name!*

# ANGELS AND PROPHETIC PROMISES

> **WE DECREE** angels who cause God's promises to materialize—be loosed.

Luke 1 recounts the story of Zacharias and Elisabeth. Zacharias was a Jewish priest serving God in the temple. He and his wife Elisabeth were old and barren. They desperately wanted to have children and had prayed for such for years. One day, as Zacharias was burning incense in the sanctuary, an angel appeared to him.

> *And when Zacharias saw him, he was troubled, and fear fell upon him. But the angel said unto him, Fear not, Zacharias: for thy prayer is heard; and thy wife Elisabeth shall bear thee a son, and thou shalt call his name John. And thou shalt have joy and gladness; and many shall rejoice at his birth* (Luke 1:12-14 KJV).

You would think that Zacharias would have been ecstatic, jumping, and dancing. Finally, God had answered their prayer! Instead, Zacharias began to question the angel about what was said, provoking him:

> *And the angel answering said unto him, I am Gabriel, that stand in the presence of God; and am sent to speak unto thee, and to shew thee these glad tidings. And, behold, thou shalt be dumb, and not able to speak, until the day that these things shall be performed, because thou believest not my words, which shall be fulfilled in their season* (Luke 1:19-20 KJV).

Zacharias was immediately stricken mute and remained unable to speak until John was born.

Gabriel was on an assignment from the Godhead. It was time for Messiah to be born, and Gabriel was the angel assigned to facilitate Christ's incarnation upon the earth. He was over it all from Mary to the shepherds on the hillside. He had a lot to do! He did not have time for Zacharias' unbelief. Zacharias' unbelief chafed Gabriel, so he "hit the mute button." There was no time for games; Jesus was coming!

It is better to say nothing than to speak unbelief and provoke angels assigned to bring about God's promises in your life. It is better to say nothing than to complain and be negative. Gabriel knew that unless he could stop Zacharias from speaking doubt and unbelief the objective would not come to pass. John would have to come through someone else. Therefore, Zacharias was muted for nine months. Gabriel knew the power of a person's words. He knew the power that man's words carried. So he acted in order to prevent Zacharias' words of doubt from interfering with God's plan. *We must get a revelation of how important our actions and our words are where angels and the promises of God are concerned.*

### LORD JESUS,

*I repent now of any time that I've chosen to complain and be negative rather than respond to You with faith and trust. Thank You that Your angels protect Your words over my life. I ask for Your grace to agree with Your promises in both word and action.*

# ANGELS AND THE NEW CAMPAIGN OF KING JESUS

> **WE DECREE** the generations are rowing together and angel armies are assisting Holy Spirit's campaign to bring in the greatest harvest of souls that has ever been seen.

In the days of Pentecost, a new move of God was about to begin. The saints needed to be prepared and empowered to be Kingdom extensions on the earth, for the King Himself was issuing the order. These 120, filled with divine empowerment from the Holy Spirit, turned the world upside down. They first affected their city, then their region, followed by heathen areas, and ultimately the uttermost parts of the earth. All of this was made possible because they recognized they were living in a new season that required mighty exploits.

Like the days of Pentecost, the angel activity happening now is certainly ushering in another campaign unlike anything before in church history. The definition of *campaign*: a series of connected activities to get or do something, organized action to obtain a purpose, or a series of related military operations. The Holy Spirit is organizing Kingdom extensions to obtain heavenly purposes, preparing for His activity and the biggest move of God in history. It is now time for the Third Great Awakening—the revival prophesied Joel. In Joel 2:25, the Lord promises to restore the years the locust have eaten away. He will restore our last harvest!

In this new campaign, the young and the old are going to participate together and operate with a transgenerational anointing. A new outpouring of the Holy Spirit is beginning with fresh anointing for members of the remnant. Although 500 people were told to go to that upper room, only 120 did. The remaining 380 had something better to do. Only those who will do what He said (the remnant) are qualified for this new anointing.

Holy Spirit is also coming to energize the remnant by releasing fresh anointings on the fivefold ministry—apostles, prophets, evangelists, pastors, and teachers. They must be refreshed and fired up for the new campaign. The calling is similar to that in Acts 1 and 2—extend Christ's Kingdom locally, regionally, and worldwide. Angels have come with Holy Spirit to assist in making that happen.

They are working to shift the church into harvest mode. Can the world be turned upside down again? Yes. Just as Joshua and the people of God shifted from forty years of wilderness wandering into their promised land assisted by the host of angels, the *tsebaah*, just as the early church shifted from the Old Testament mindset to a New Testament power-filled Kingdom mindset assisted by the *tsebaah*—so it is today. We are now shifting into a new campaign of King Jesus, and we will likewise be assisted by the same *tsebaah*. The charismatic movement is over. It is now time for the apostolic campaign of King Jesus on this earth. Multitudes in the valley of decision are going to be brought in. Harvests are going to be restored sevenfold. A new move of the Holy Spirit is coming to the New Testament churches, and the angel army network is assisting in empowering the remnant to participate. As the Holy Spirit is organizing a new campaign to obtain God's purposes, His workers, saints, and the angelic network are to yield in full obedience to prepare and participate.

## HOLY SPIRIT,

*Thank You that a fresh move of Your glory is coming now and the campaign of King Jesus is being established in the earth. I yield to this move of Your Spirit and pray for a renewed sense of surrender as You bring about the greatest harvest of souls the world has ever seen!*

# ANGELS AND HOLY SPIRIT OUTPOURINGS

> **WE DECREE** angels assisting the Holy Spirit and fresh outpourings—be loosed. We ask You, Lord, loose Holy Spirit's fire among us. Loose it today. Loose it here.

Acts 2:3 says on the day of Pentecost, cloven tongues of fire sat upon everyone in the upper room. All 120 had a flame over them, a cloven tongue of fire. Now remember that a divine shift was taking place as the church was transitioning to a different level. It was moving from the old covenant to a new level of authority and ministry. When that shift began, cloven tongues of fire, accompanied by the Holy Spirit, sat upon them. Angels ministered this fire to each believer so they would be empowered for the new campaign. Angels accompanying Holy Spirit were firing up the saints to move. This was to be a fired-up movement. The key to any movement is movement. Holy Spirit and His angels were clearly saying, *"Fire up and move!"*

This is what has been happening in recent times with increased angelic activity. Angels are even now ministering to help release a fresh outpouring of the Holy Spirit. One of their assignments is to bring fresh fire to believers under Holy Spirit supervision, to spiritually set them on fire. Ezekiel 1:13 begins this doctrine by describing angels as having the appearance of burning coals of fire, like the appearance of lamps that went up and down among the living creatures. The angels appeared as flashes of light, or *pur*, cloven tongues of fire. The Bible in Basic English says that between the living beings it looked as if flames were chasing after each other across burning coals of fire. This is exactly what it looked like on the day of Pentecost as bright fire flashed on top of the 120 believers! What was happening? Angels were ministering fresh fire from God's altar upon them. The angel network was accompanying the Holy Spirit, the other "self "of Christ, assisting in shifting the church to a new level of ministry.

It is time for a new outpouring. It is time for the church to receive fresh power from on high. It is time for fresh fire upon all believers. It is time for a divine shift to take the church to new levels. It is time for the apostles and believers to begin affecting their regions with the Gospel, as angels under Holy Spirit supervision network with the church. They are moving now upon fresh Holy Spirit winds to assist the saints to do the same works Jesus did. They are flashing about as lightning.

We are entering into the greatest time in human history, in which the remnant is about to see God activity as it has never been seen before. The days that we have been praying forth for years have already begun; thus, we must get into step with them. We are not waiting on God; He is waiting on us. When the angel touched Isaiah's lips, the question was, "Who will go for us?" All God is listening for is, "Here am I, God. I'll go." Like the 500 who were instructed to gather in the upper room, you have to choose to either participate in God's Kingdom extension on the earth or to miss out on the greatest revival the world has ever seen.

## LORD JESUS,

*As a fresh move of Your Spirit is being poured out on the earth, loose Your angels to partner with what Heaven is doing here and now. I ask for a fresh touch of Your fire to fall upon me, my family and my region. I long to participate in what You are doing. Come, Holy Spirit!*

# THE CHURCH,
# A MOVEMENT

> **WE DECREE** Holy Spirit is now supervising
> a new movement of awesome revival.

Why the increase of angelic activity in recent times? Why the increase of signs and wonders in the heavens? I believe it's a confirming sign that it is time for a new campaign of Holy Spirit. Over the past decade we have heard key after key after key concerning the success of an apostolic campaign, but we have been missing the most basic key to all apostolic movements. *The key to any movement is "movement."* You have to move. You cannot always be on vacation. There are times when you must engage. There are some times when you've got to display the courage of a Gideon and stand up in the culture to make a difference. You can't always run and hide. Sometimes you have to engage and go get something that was stolen from you. It's time for the church to arise and take back what's been stolen from us.

It is time in this moment for the people of God to become engaged. Angels are networking with the church under Holy Spirit supervision and they are striking the enemies of our King and His Kingdom. Angels are bringing coals from the altar of Heaven to try and fire up the people of God. Holy Spirit is moving to release power for a new beginning, a new outpouring, and a new season to be fruitful and multiply. He is coming to resurrect and renew a movement, not an institution. We are called to be a part of a movement like the 120 in the upper room who turned our world upside down with a Gospel of the Kingdom.

Movements do not sit or stand around dazed and confused, wondering what is going on and why God isn't taking things back from the devil for them. They get up and they start to move, knowing that if they move, all of Heaven will move with them. It's time for the church to get up and move in the power of the Holy Spirit. It's time to move in signs, wonders, and miracles. It's time to move in the gifts of the Holy Spirit again—words of wisdom, gifts of faith, discerning of spirits, healings, and miracles. The church by definition is to be a movement. It is time for the church of the King to begin to move from complacency to focused Christianity. From intimidation to great valor. From hopelessness to faith and confidence in the living God. To move from the four walls into the streets and the marketplace, into government and the media, into business, education, arts, and entertainment. From selfish, "what's in it for me" Christianity to servants of God doing His will. From consumer Christianity to discipleship.

## GOD,

*Empower Your church for the fresh campaign of King Jesus that You are releasing now. May Your Bride be readied, filled with fresh fire, and emboldened for the movement that is taking place. May we be the movement, sparking fresh revival throughout the world as we engage with culture to represent You well.*

# STICKY FAVOR

> **WE DECREE** the sticky favor
> of God is all over Christ's heirs!

The angelic assistance that we need in Heaven is quite different than the angelic assistance we need now.

On this side of Heaven, we need angels who excel in strength, perform God's Word, bring God's promises to pass, and assist us in our position of reigning with Christ on the earth.

Romans 5:17 declares that we are to reign in life. We cannot reign in life to the degree that we should unless angels assist us. Psalm 103:21 says that angels do God's good pleasure. *Pleasure* is the Hebrew word *ratson*. It means "goodwill, desire, inclination, grace and favor" (Strong, H7522). *Ratson* means "concrete reaction of a superior to an inferior." Jesus the King is superior. He has far more authority than we do and reigns in far greater measure. But in His name believers can reign in life. Angels are sent to help Christ's heirs do exactly that.

Proverbs 14:35 (KJV) says, *"The king's favour is toward a wise servant: but his wrath is against him that causeth shame."*

The King's goodwill—or favor, *ratson*—is toward us and it is grace given. It is also administered, in some ways, by angels. The angels minister the goodwill of Jesus to us in *concrete* ways, not phantom ways. King Jesus, the superior one, has commanded the angel armies to do His good pleasure toward you and me. It's a rock-solid promise in our lives. It's a benefit that King David sings about in Psalm 103:2 that we are to never forget. Don't forget that angels are assigned to minister God's goodwill to you in real ways.

The Hebrew idea behind *ratson* is "concrete." It solidly materializes. Concrete involves union with something that is material or actual and it means "cohesion to form a mass." King David says angels are amassing God's goodwill that is *solidly real* to materialize and adhere or stick to us. The goodwill of Christ sticks with you. It's not fragile or hit and miss. It is something you can stand on because it's concrete. Angels cause the blessings of God to materialize in concrete ways.

King David says God's favor toward His heirs is sticky. It's a sticky benefit. If I were to have a jar of honey and pour someone a handful of it, you would find out it's sticky. God's favor is sticky! Have you ever met someone who is "sticky" with favor? It just seems all they do is blessed. That is how God wants all His heirs to live. He wants all His benefits sticking to them and working His good pleasure. *Benefit* is the Hebrew word *gemuwl*. It means "to reward or to treat well" (Strong, H1576). A business that provides benefits to its employees does so to treat them well. Most certainly God treats His heirs, the born-again ones, very well. We are His heirs and His angels are sent to reward us with tangible material blessings that are concrete.

## LORD JESUS,

*Thank You that the assistance of Your angels prepares me to reign in life with You. I receive the ministry of the angelic now and posture my heart to receive new measures of Your favor. As Your angels minster Your goodwill and blessing toward me, my heart responds with gratitude.*

# The Kingdom Number

> **WE DECREE** we have far more righteous angels on our side than demons against us. The natural number is not the Kingdom number.

Colossians 1:18 and 2:10 name Christ as head over every power and authority, which includes all principalities and dominions. He is the preeminent one; He is above all powers, might, and dominions. This refers to both angelic and demonic powers. We should always remember that the kingdom of darkness simply counterfeits God's organized Kingdom in operation and rank.

There are millions of these angel warriors, fellow servants who are assisting us. Hebrews 12:22 says, it is *"an innumerable company of angels"* (NKJV). Only one-third of the angels fell when lucifer rebelled (see Rev. 12:4). That leaves two-thirds of the angels left on our side unless God has created more angels. This means there are far more angels for us than fallen angels against us. It is at least two to one. That should add to the confidence of the overcomers, the remnant warriors.

Sometimes in the natural realm we are very outnumbered. Sometimes the odds against us are incredibly high off the charts. There are some today who say you will never see an awakening or revival in the United States, because the odds are just too high. Sometimes the number in the natural realm looks impossible. But the natural number is not the Kingdom number! The Kingdom number is overwhelmingly in our favor. We've got to understand that. God is with us, Holy Spirit is with us, Messiah the Breaker goes before us, and millions of His angels are standing with us to implement strategy, plans, and laws to protect, to steward the resources, and to enforce covenants.

In Second Kings 6 the prophet Elisha and his servant found themselves surrounded by the Syrian army. They were incredibly outnumbered by the army and its war chariots, and Elisha's servant cried out to Elisha in Second Kings 6:15, *What shall we do?*

Elisha's response was, "Relax. There's more on our side than on their side." So Elisha's servant takes a head count—"one, two." Two was the natural number, but it wasn't the Kingdom number. Elisha prayed, "Lord, open his eyes." And when his servant's spiritual eyes were opened, he saw that the hillsides were filled with God's angel army. Horses, chariots of fire, and angels arrayed for battled surrounded them.

God gave miraculous victory in the face of overwhelming odds. Is the remnant number enough to see the greatest days in church history? Is the remnant number enough to see a worldwide revival? Is it enough to change this nation? Yes, because the natural number is not the Kingdom number. There are far more with us than with our adversary. God the Father, God the Son Jesus, the Holy Spirit, and millions of His angels are on our side. If the remnant will step forward into battle, though we see odds that are too great for us we will see the mighty army of the Kingdom of God come to our rescue. The shock and awe is not on the natural side, it is on the spiritual side. Far more than enough sides with us to give us victory.

### JESUS,

*Thank You that You, the Breaker, go before me! Thank You that the Kingdom number is always greater than the natural number. Please open my eyes so that I may see that more are with me than with my adversary and victory is on the way!*

# ANGELS' RESPONSE TO GOD'S WORD

**WE DECREE** we will prophesy the Word of the Lord.

Psalm 103:20 (NKJV) says, *"Bless the Lord, you His angels, who excel in strength, who do His word, heeding the voice of His word."*

The Hebrew word for *heeding* is *shama*, which means "to come to attention like a soldier, to perceive intelligently and obey, and to give undivided attention for the purpose of obeying or fulfilling" (Strong, H8085). Angels stand to attention when the Word of the Lord is declared. They heed it. Sons and daughters speak the voice of God's Word on this earth. When we speak the Scriptures, we are speaking God's Word. When we make decrees, angels snap to attention to bring that Word to pass. They don't hearken to our word; they hearken to and obey the Word of God that we declare.

An angel network is laboring to bring about the decrees of the saints, the bold declarations of Scripture. They circle around Holy Spirit-led worship. By implication, an assistant or a helper helps someone do something. Angels help us do things in the Kingdom, but they do not do our work for us. They are not slaves; they are assistants. In other words, it is expected that *you* do something. Angels do not help those who do nothing. They are not assisting the passive, uninvolved, uncommitted, lackadaisical, or lukewarm Christian. You must be a doer of the Word to tap into Heaven's network. Do something and watch the assistance start. Be a doer, actively engaged in Kingdom advancement locally, regionally, and throughout the world. Be engaged against the powers of hell. Don't just talk about prayer, but be a doer of the Word after praying the Word.

If we give our time, talent, and finances, angels will assist us. The two areas in which you will see the most angelic activity are worship and prayer. Worship is a form of song decrees, while prayer is heart decrees to God. The unifying factor here is that we must be people who decree the Word of God to activate angels.

The alarm clock of Heaven is ringing on the nightstand of a sleeping church. It is time for us to rise to the occasion. The "watchers," or angels, are watching for us *to do* something. Are you doing what God says? Are you a doer of the Word or a forgetful hearer?

James 1:22-24 (KJV) says, *"But be ye doers of the word, and not hearers only, deceiving your own selves. For if any be a hearer of the word, and not a doer, he is like unto a man beholding his natural face in a glass: for he beholdeth himself, and goeth his way, and straightway forgetteth what manner of man he was."*

Do not forget who you are. You are a King's son or daughter. You are a person of authority, here to rule and reign in life through Jesus Christ. You are here to be a participant in the King's Third Great Awakening. Do something for the King and the angels will assist you.

## LORD,

*As Your sons and daughters declare Your Word, may Your angels swiftly bring it to pass. Remind me today, Lord, of Your prophetic promises and Scriptures that I may meditate on and decree them into the atmosphere. I want to be a doer of Your Word, not a forgetful hearer.*

# THE POWER OF DECREES

> **WE DECREE** the remnant church will declare what God says. Angels are moving with power to bring God's Word to pass.

*You shall also decide and decree a thing, and it shall be established for you; and the light [of God's favor] shall shine upon your ways* (Job 22:28 AMP).

The word *thing* in the above verse is the Hebrew word *omer*, meaning "a word or a promise" (Strong, H562). The heirs of God and the joint heirs with Christ have authority to decree words of Scripture, words of promise, words of prophecy (which are also words of God given through Holy Spirit enlightenment). Those words, in Jesus' name, will be established. *Established* is the Hebrew word *quwm*, meaning "to be made good, to perform, succeed, to raise up and come to be or to pass" (Strong, H6965). *Quwm* is used in the Hebrew language as a construction word. When you decree a word, you are constructing it into your life. You're building it to appear on your life's pathway. It becomes performed into your life's ways; it's why words are so important. When we decree a word of the Lord, when we speak a promise, when we speak a principle or a prophecy that is based upon God's Word, His favor anoints that word to come to pass in our lives.

The word *way* is the Hebrew word *derek,* meaning "a road or a path" (Strong, H1870). It refers to the course of life, life's journey, or a way of life. When we speak a word that is based upon what God says, it's made good on our life's journey. It comes into our path and intersects our life at some point. It also rouses angel armies to assist us. Remember, Psalm 103:20 says that angels listen for God's Word that we speak. Why? To bring those words or promises to pass, to intersect them with our life and cause them to be constructed and built into our life's journey. When we speak our faith, when we say what God says, angels hearken to it and organize to make it good. They assist the heirs, the born-again ones, by helping it come to pass. Angels help construct and connect us to its fulfillment.

Decrees are like prophecy. When you decree a word, you are prophesying into the course of your life. You are prophesying your future. Angels will hearken to bring it to pass. It is vital that we pray what God says. It is vital that we declare our faith, speaking His words over our lives. Hearkening angels will begin building them into our future.

We are assisted by very patient beings, and this patience cannot be compromised. They are committed to their assignments and will faithfully stand to complete them. They do not quit. I am confident some angels have been patiently waiting, in some cases for years and even decades, for the saints to move so that they could also move. They have been waiting for the decrees necessary to go forth to change a region. They have been waiting for a remnant who would be proactive and turn things around. They have been patiently waiting for years for various individuals—maybe even you—to turn around and fire up for God so that they can assist them with their God-given destinies.

## HOLY SPIRIT,

*I decree Your word today, choosing to partner with what You have said and what You are saying. As I decree, I am acutely aware that the angelic hosts are partnering with me to see Your promises come to pass. Thank You for the patience of the angelic as they wait upon these decrees. Please give me boldness to believe You and speak Your word passionately into my life and circumstances.*

# Angel Armies and the Church's Authority

> **WE DECREE** waves of Holy Spirit enablement
> are now gathering angel armies to partner with
> the church to battle for the throne of their region.

Remember, one of the duties of the ekklesia in Jesus' day was to summon and release armies. They had authority to release the army of the region should war be necessary. It is time for the church to pray and summon angel armies to help them cleanse the heavens over them. Ephesians 6:12 (KJV), *"For we wrestle not against flesh and blood, but against principalities, against powers, against the rulers of the darkness of this world, against spiritual wickedness in high places."*

We are to put on our armor, as the rest of Ephesians 6 describes, and battle for the throne of the region and disciple it. Jesus promised that the authorities of hell would not prevail against His church. We will see a church that confronts these demon princes and demonic strongholds that hinder the coming forth of the Kingdom of God. There is going to be an aggressive church that is going to rise up and say, "No, nothing between me and God. Nothing between earth and Heaven."

The church that understands her authority is going to take her seat in heavenly places and govern for King Jesus by the decrees she makes. They are going to verbalize a "yes" or a "no" to laws and cultural values within their regions.

Holy Spirit is synergizing the generations together with a fresh anointing of power. He is adding to it angel armies. The battle for the throne of regions is going to be won by the heirs of God and the joint heirs with Christ who have ears to hear what the Spirit of God is saying.

We are living at the end of an age with awesome promise. We are not here to be a weak, emaciated, silent body. We are not here to be governed by hell. We are here to dominate hell with superior authority. Awesome days are opening up before us.

The prophetic word from the Scriptures is very bold. The church is to rise and sit with Christ in heavenly places. It is to overrule and overthrow demon powers in a region and occupy the spiritual throne to such a degree that it affects the function of the earthly government beneath it. Christ wants His preeminence in all regions. The church (the ekklesia) is to rule and reign with Christ. We are here to occupy the throne of a territory and declare God's way.

The ekklesia is to rule and reign with Christ in the spiritual realms over a region and in the natural realms. It's both. Visible or invisible doesn't matter. Natural thrones or spiritual thrones—doesn't matter. Natural dominion or spiritual dominion, it doesn't matter. Natural power or spiritual power—doesn't matter. Why? So that in the visible or the invisible regions, Christ has the preeminence. We are being challenged to step forward and accept an assignment that the church has neglected for decades. It is time to hear the call of King Jesus: *I will have a people who will rise to sit with Me in seats of authority. They will displace demon princes and refuse to allow them to reign any longer.*

## LORD JESUS,

*Come and have Your way in my region. May Your Kingdom be established here and now in the earth! I pray for Your ekklesia to rise to her rightful place of authority, to rule and reign with You. I put on Your full armor today, believing in faith for my region to be ruled by the rightful king, King Jesus.*

# Warfare Strategies

**WE DECREE** angels who assist prophetic promises to come to pass—be loosed in Jesus' name. Bring them to us; accelerate them.

Psalm 103:20 (NLT) says, *"Praise the Lord, you angels, you mighty ones who carry out his plans, listening for each of his commands."* This means they listen and respond to the words of God that we speak (including Holy Spirit-inspired prophetic words and decrees of faith) organizing, fighting, and campaigning to bring them to pass. They are heavenly warriors.

In Judges 13 an angel came to Manoah and his wife. She was barren, but the angel said they were going to have a son. He even told her what she was to eat and drink. The prophetic word came to pass, and she did have a son and named him Samson.

In the often-read Christmas story, Mary was given a prophetic word. The angel Gabriel said, "You're going to have the prophesied Messiah." Gabriel even repeated the prophecy of Isaiah 7:14 to Mary, *"A virgin shall conceive, and bear a son."* The angel knew the prophetic word and he was bringing it to pass.

First Timothy 1:18 says that prophetic words are to be used as warfare strategies. I have used this all over the state of Ohio. When I hold prayer assemblies in one of our 88 counties, I start with prophetic words to our region. This sparks faith for breakthrough. Also, Judges 13:3 shows us that angels help those prophetic words come to pass. What vital assistance! I have no doubt angels have done that for us in Ohio. Our apostolic council meets to pray over prophetic words we receive and then we develop ways to implement the prophecies into our region. This has helped us shift our state toward great awakening. This has also released angel armies to assist us. Our testimony is clear—angels have assisted us to help change our region.

Angels have helped us overcome Jezebel and religious spirits that have caused great barrenness in the past. Angels have partnered with us in shifting Ohio from a spiritually dry desert to one ripe for revival. Great revival is now being stirred throughout our region because of promises God's people have been decreeing in every county and over 600 churches. Angels have been hearkening to those prophetic words and warring alongside of us for their fulfillment.

Many of us have been given prophetic words. If you have received a prophetic word, decree it in the name of the Lord. Angels are here to assist in bringing prophetic promises to pass. Many of the prophetic promises that have come to you are not going to happen without angelic assistance. We have to decree, pray, and loose them.

### JESUS,

*Thank You that Your angels are privy to Your promises over our lives and work alongside of us to see them fulfilled. Today, remind me of prophetic words over my life that I may decree them into the atmosphere and see them come to pass. I welcome the angelic to come—I decree, pray and loose them into their assignments.*

# EXPECT THE ANGELS

> **WE DECREE** we will see more angel activity than demon activity. We forbid demon activity in Jesus' name.

Many today, I believe, are missing out on some awesome benefits because they are not giving voice to God's Word. Often, they are voicing anything and everything *except* God's Word. The angels are waiting for you to say things that loose them. The key is to speak the Word of God.

The reason that much of the body of Christ today sees more demonic activity than angel activity is because they activate more demons than they do angels. It's amazing to me how conditioned and accepting much of the body of Christ is today to demonic strategies and activities. It's almost as though the body of Christ expects demons to move against them. They expect the kingdom of hell to fight them at every turn. They expect hell's obstacles and hindering demons. Yes, we know demons are here to steal, kill, and destroy. Why not renew our minds to the fact that we have far more assisters helping us to win than we have resisters who are causing us to lose? Why not expect Holy Spirit and His angels to come to our aid? Why not expect angel armies to have a better strategy than demons have? Why not expect our leader, Jesus, and His angels to be more powerful and wiser than fallen angels that were dumb enough to follow lucifer? Our angels thought God was more powerful than lucifer. Why not decree and expect the Kingdom of Almighty God to surround us with protection and deliverance? Why shouldn't the church expect more angelic activity than demonic activity?

It's time to recondition our minds to truth and reposition our thoughts. It's time to get up in the morning looking for angels instead of demons. Yes, demons and hell's kingdom are real, but so are angels and our Kingdom. Our angels are stronger and smarter than hell's demons, and we have more of them. But far more than that, our God, our King, our Lord is exceedingly, abundantly, above and beyond, more powerful than lucifer ever thought about being. It's time to act like it and stop thinking in line with our fallen nature.

We aren't fallen anymore. We are born-again heirs. It's time to believe and stop thinking like unrighteous sinners and start thinking like the heirs of God. The culture of defeat that has been propagated by the body of Christ for decades is delusional. It makes no sense biblically. We aren't fallen-down wimps who are demon dominated. We are seated with Christ in heavenly places. We are heirs with authority to rule and reign. Loose your angels! Expect angel armies fighting on your side! Expect to win!

I expect the Greater One to give us strategy to overcome. I expect to win. I expect that we are going to get strategy that overcomes all the powers of the adversary. I expect angels to be loosed.

## HOLY SPIRIT,

*I ask for You to come and renew my mind today. Bring transformation to my heart that I may have a fresh expectation for the angelic in my life and circumstances. May my expectation match the truth that You are the Greater One!*

# Understanding the Times

> **WE DECREE** Holy Spirit is breathing
> life into our King's campaign.

In First Chronicles 12:32, the sons of Issachar both discerned the times and gained understanding of what Israel ought to do. In following their example of searching the season out, I feel it is vital to provide pertinent doctrinal foundations to help us discern the times in which we now live. Foundational truths add credibility to current kingdom activity and thus activate greater faith and confidence within us. They simultaneously refresh and refocus us.

Let us examine the Hebrew roots of some words that will be important as we learn to discern the time:

- *Biynah* (understand): knowledge, wisdom, insight, intelligence (Strong, H998)
- *Eth* (times): the proper time or right season for an event to happen (Strong, H6256)
- *Yada* (know): to perceive, to anoint to see clearly, to inform, or to reveal; knowledge gained through the senses (to sense); to distinguish between options (Strong, H3045)
- *Asah* (ought to do): to execute, work, create or build; to prepare; describes God's creative activities (our implication is to prepare for God's activities) (Strong, H6213)
- Rhema words: Holy Spirit revealed revelation and enlightenment from the Scriptures

Understanding the Hebrew roots of these words prepares us for the release of revelation and *biynah* understanding. Remembering and meditating on such teaching, as well as the prophetic words we've received, allows *asah* to happen. It gives us intelligence and wisdom, revealing the appropriate time and action for an event that has come into season. It anoints us with perception to sense and distinguish the proper option so that it can be executed in work, and so that we can appropriately prepare for the release of God's creative activity into a "happening." In other words, past teachings and prophetic words coupled with present understanding of the times is vital for wisdom to flow and vision to be carried out at the right time.

It is time we rethink teachings, rethink prophetic words, in order to refocus our attention and increase wisdom for the now. This activates faith and confidence, giving us wisdom and intelligence for this season of God's creative activity.

In Acts 1 and 2, we read the last promise Jesus made to His disciples—indeed, the last statement He made before ascending into Heaven. He prophesied the coming of the Holy Spirit. It was the appropriate time for Him to come; it was the *eth,* so they would be filled with power from on high.

In Acts 1:4 and 8, Jesus told His disciples not to leave Jerusalem until the Holy Spirit came and filled them. He was giving them this type of power to be His witnesses in Jerusalem (their city), Judea (their region), Samaria (heathen areas), and to the uttermost parts of the world.

The 120 believers, who gathered in the upper room following this instruction, were used to facilitate the new Kingdom campaign Christ wanted to release on earth. We, as believers, must be open and yearning for the power of the Holy Spirit to operate through our lives to extend the Kingdom of God on the earth, as did the 120 in the upper room, so that a new campaign can be carried out.

## LORD JESUS,

*I recognize that I need a fresh touch of Your Holy Spirit. Just as the 120 postured themselves to receive a baptism of power, I posture my heart today. I yield to You, Lord, knowing that as the Holy Spirit empowers me, the Kingdom of God will be extended on the earth.*

# Activating the Heir Force

**WE DECREE** the Heir Force is loosed (the assisters of the heirs of Christ). In Jesus' name, we deploy them.

*Are they not all ministering spirits, sent forth to minister for them who shall be heirs of salvation?* (Hebrews 1:14 KJV)

About ten years ago, I began to think about the various networks that are evident in our nation, especially those of apostolic and prophetic nature. There has been a vast effort to organize (network) the apostles and the prophets into this new campaign God wants to do right now.

As I was thinking about where I fit in all of it, what my involvement ought to be—what I should be doing—and the various networks in general, the Holy Spirit spoke to me in a way that has now guided me in several directions. He asked me very clearly, *"What about My angel network?"* The Holy Spirit has a way of asking and making a statement at the same time. All of a sudden, I was riveted upon that phrase—*angel network*. I had never before thought of the angels as being networked. I remember pausing and thinking, "Well yeah, God didn't create millions of angels only to see if He could. He didn't say, 'Let's make some angels and see what they will do. It might be amusing.'"

Angels were made and networked for a purpose. They are disciplined into an organized army, dedicated and focused on their assignment, which is Christ's heirs. *We* are the assignment they have been given.

Romans 8:17 (NIV) says, *"Now if we are children, then we are heirs— heirs of God and co-heirs with Christ."*

One day, I drove out to the lake to pray and to think about the angel network and strategies needed to overcome narcissism in the church. As I was pulling alongside the lake, the Holy Spirit spoke another word to me. This word was very forceful and bold. Although very rare for me, He spoke this word audibly and so loudly that I had to pull the car over to the side and stop. I was shaking. The words were like a command as He boldly said, *"Release my Heir force,"* meaning "the force behind the heirs." I knew immediately He meant "heir" and not "air." That word became an apostolic assignment that I have since carried everywhere I've gone.

Just as the United States military has an air force that can be called in to rescue its own or called in to deliver blows to the enemy, this "Heir Force" can be sent to deliver a region. The church has an Heir Force organized by the Godhead to help us unlock the regions for this present-time salvation. They are organized to open up the heavens, to scatter and shatter powers of darkness encamped in regions, to thwart the strategies of hell, and to partner with apostolic teams. They are organized to assist, empower, deliver, and rescue. We have an Heir Force behind us empowered by God Himself. With it, we will affect change, bless and release provision, and make the campaign He has ordained successful. *It is time to release this Heir Force.*

### HOLY SPIRIT,

*In Jesus' name, I pray for Your angelic network, Your Heir Force, to be released. I pray that my region would experience the impact of their release and that deliverance would be a byproduct of their coming. I ask for an open Heaven. I ask for the powers of darkness to be scattered and shattered. May Your Heir Force come now!*

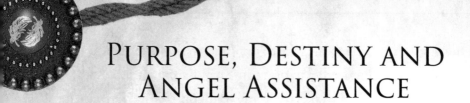

# Purpose, Destiny and Angel Assistance

> **WE DECREE** angels who assist Holy Spirit in leading God's plan for our lives before we were ever born—be loosed in Jesus' name.

Our destiny and purpose are God provided and were designed before we were ever born. There are certain aspects of my destiny that I will never achieve without the Holy Spirit. Romans 8:14 says that we must be led by the Spirit to manifest the fact that we are sons and daughters of the living God. I need the power and support of the Holy Spirit or there are aspects of my destiny I will never accomplish.

There are some things about my destiny that God in His wisdom decreed the angels would assist. This is New Testament doctrine—God's plan. He sent the angels to assist us. It is His will.

Angels briefed and assigned to assist our destiny is revealed throughout the Scriptures. In Luke 1:30, the angel Gabriel knew that Mary was to be the mother of Jesus. He knew that was her destiny before she did. Gabriel actually revealed this to her and was there to help bring it to pass. Obviously, he was briefed on her destiny before he ever showed up. His words and actions would not have been possible any other way.

Luke 1 also tells us the testimony of the high priest Zacharias and his wife Elizabeth. They were physically unable to have children, but barrenness was not their destiny. The angel Gabriel appeared to Zacharias one day and revealed God's plan for his life. It was Zacharias and Elizabeth's destiny to have a son, and the angel of the Lord revealed that destiny to them. The angel clearly knew it before they did.

The angel also knew John's destiny although he was not yet born. There was not one cell to John's life yet. It had just been prophesied that he would come into being. Though yet unborn, the angel knew John was to be like Elijah.

In Acts 27 we read that the apostle Paul was a prisoner on a ship traveling to Italy when a fierce storm arose. It soon became evident that the ship was going to be destroyed. Just before this happened the angel of the Lord appeared to Paul and told him not to be afraid because he must be brought before Caesar. He gave Paul a destiny word. The angel knew it was God's plan for him to go to Rome and appear before Caesar. Because of Paul's prayer and obedience, angels were released to tend to that destiny, conducting a miraculous rescue at sea whereby Paul and everyone on board made it safely to land.

Notice the angel said to him, "You must get to Rome." *Must* is the Greek word *dei* meaning "necessary by the nature of something, obliged, personal obligation, or unavoidable" (Strong, G1163). The angel said, "This is not avoidable. You have to get to Rome." This is a destiny assignment. In Acts 27:24 (NABRE) the angel said, *"Do not be afraid, Paul. You are destined to stand before Caesar."* Don't be afraid— you have a destiny appointment. By the angel revealing himself to Paul, the angel was assuring him, "The angel armies are behind you, and they are going to get you to Rome."

### JESUS,

*Your angels know the plans and purposes You have for my life. I believe they are working now to see my destiny come to pass. Thank You that even before I was born, You made a way and wrote my story. I confess I need the power and support of Your Holy Spirit and Your angels to see my destiny fulfilled!*

# DEFINE THE CULTURE

> **WE DECREE** in Jesus' name, we (the heirs, the ekklesia, the church) overthrow demon powers in this region and nation. Lord Sabbaoth, the Lord of angel armies, is on our side. We will win!

*For unto us a child is born, unto us a son is given: and the government shall be upon his shoulder: and his name shall be called Wonderful, Counsellor, The mighty God, The ever- lasting Father, The Prince of Peace. Of the increase of his government and peace there shall be no end, upon the throne of David, and upon his kingdom, to order it, and to establish it with judgment and with justice from henceforth even forever. The zeal of the Lord of hosts [angel armies] will perform this (Isaiah 9:6-7 KJV).*

The word *government* is the Hebrew word *misrah*, meaning "empire or dynasty" (Strong, H4951). Jesus wants His church representing His throne and extending His empire into the territories of their region. *Throne* is the Hebrew word *kicceh*, and it means "the seat of power; seat of authority; canopy under which rule extends; jurisdiction of a position of honor, and the position from which a king reigns" (Strong, H3678). Jesus sits upon the throne of His Kingdom to order it, establishing judgment and justice. He wants His church aligning with Him to accomplish that rule.

The zeal of Lord Sabaoth, the Lord of angel armies, will perform this. Angel armies will partner with and assist the church in battling for the "throne" and in establishing Christ's Kingdom in their region. Jesus will release His armies to assist the church, who obeys His commands, in binding or loosing some things on earth. This is clearly seen in Christ's name for the church, the Greek word *ekklesia*. It is used 113 times in the New Testament, and it is a political word, not a religious word" (Strong, G1577). You would think that Jesus would use a religious word, such as *temple* or *synagogue*, but He doesn't. By calling His church *ekklesia*, He uses a word describing the act of governing.

*Perform* is the Hebrew word *asah* meaning "to work, to procure something, to accomplish, to construct, and to build." *Asah* is also translated in Judges 11:36 as "to make war" (Strong, H6213). Angel armies will make war with hell's kingdom, on the church's behalf, to enforce its "bindings" or its "loosing" decrees. Angels help procure regions. They help us build a kingdom "hub" or "stronghold" according to the decrees that are made by heirs of the region in Jesus' name. The angel armies of Lord Sabaoth will be "loosed" to help the church increase Christ's Kingdom's influence throughout the region.

The church is to decree the laws, judgments, plans, purposes, and principles of God's Word *to* principalities and powers in the heavenly places. The church, not hell's kingdom, is to define the message and culture of a region. King Jesus commanded that. And if demons get in the way, He says to cast them down and ask for angel armies. The *ekklesia* is to occupy the throne of their region and give an uncompromised Gospel, insisting that the will of God be done in that region and battle with hell to see that it stays that way.

## JESUS,

*You are the Lord Sabaoth, the Lord of angel armies. There is no higher King than You. I declare that Your laws and judgments, plans and purposes are coming to pass in my region and in my generation. May Your ekklesia arise now to declare Your Word into our culture, bringing great change and establishing the Kingdom of Heaven.*

# ANGELS AND PROSPERITY

> **WE DECREE** angels who connect us to places, people, events, business, material properties, sales, jobs, and job promotions that prosper us—be loosed in Jesus' name.

If we believe that the devil and the kingdom of darkness can hinder the blessings of God from entering our lives, then why wouldn't we believe that Christ's angels can assist in releasing them? If the heavenly hosts are connected to a giving God, then why wouldn't we believe they have the ability to release blessings upon us? The Scriptures are clear—angels avidly assist us in obtaining resources, finances, and other benefits to help us in establishing God's Kingdom here on the earth.

Angels connect God's people to places, people, events, businesses, sales, and material property that will prosper them. It is a part of the angels' assignment where born-again ones, heirs of Christ, are concerned. It's a fascinating principle all over the Old and New Testament that is rarely ever mentioned or taught. It's a magnificent benefit that we are told we should not ever forget.

In Acts 10, an angel appears to a Gentile, a Roman army officer of the Italian regiment by the name of Cornelius. When the angel appeared to him, he made note of Cornelius' prayer life and financial stewardship. Of all the things an angel might address, someone's giving record would not seem to be a priority. But the angel said to Cornelius in Acts 10:4 (NKJV), *"Your prayers and your alms have come up for a memorial before God."*

The Greek word for *memorial, mnemosunon,* means "a reminder, a record, to rehearse something, make mention, or to bring to remembrance" (Strong, G3422). A memorial draws your attention to some- thing that needs to be remembered. It tells us about a life-changing event through the medium of chiseled stone.

In referring to Cornelius' memorial, the Angel of the Lord says, "Cornelius, your giving record has come up before God and it has His attention. It has been talked about in the throne room, Cornelius. God is rehearsing your giving history. Your offerings have been remembered before God." Then the angel said to him, "I want you to send men to Joppa and ask for the apostle Peter to come to your house."

Peter continued with them to Cornelius' house, where he preached the Gospel of salvation through faith in Jesus Christ. In Acts 10:44 (NLT), Luke says, *"Even as Peter was saying these things, the Holy Spirit fell upon all who were listening to the message."* Everyone in Cornelius' house was saved and filled with the Holy Spirit. *What a blessing.* It's an eternal blessing of far greater value than any other blessing. It is because of Cornelius' prayers and offerings that angels were able to work in his life and his family's life. His offerings got the attention of God and His angels, who are sent forth to minister to the heirs of salvation. As Christians, we must understand that one of the ministries of angels is to connect us to the blessings of Christ, as well as to assist in prospering us.

## HOLY SPIRIT,

*Thank You that Your angels are assisting me now to bring me into places of great blessing and favor with You. I welcome Your angels to connect me to people, places and opportunities to bring new measures of prosperity in my life and in the lives of those that I care about.*

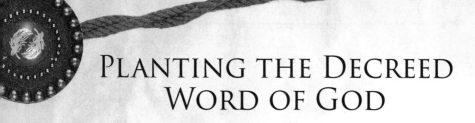

# PLANTING THE DECREED WORD OF GOD

> **WE DECREE** the earth is being seeded now with the decreed word of God.

*Words are seeds.* I was reading Genesis 1—the awesome description of God creating the heavens and the earth. Suddenly, I heard the voice of Holy Spirit so clearly. *Words are seeds.* His voice was heavy with meaning, with *instruction.*

How many times had I read Genesis 1, penned by Moses 3,400 years ago? Countless times. But this time I leaned back from my desk, echoing aloud what was recorded in ancient history thousands of years ago. I knew Holy Spirit was giving me a truth that is still alive, still powerful, and still needs to be loosed. It was a moment of enlightenment, and I would never be the same after that revelation.

Words are seeds. "Word seeds" germinate and they grow. "Word seeds," planted properly, reproduce themselves. "Word seeds" are the concealed beginnings of something that can grow to fullness when we believe and act upon them. They are latent potential, waiting to be planted in the soil of an individual, a church, a business, or a nation that can grow and fulfill that "word seed."

We are told that God planted the heavens and the earth with word seeds—words that became what He decreed. Heaven and earth became what He seeded, decreed, and described with His words. From the beginning God was sharing with man, who was made in His image and likeness, how they could partner with Him and be creators by decreeing word seeds. We do not create from nothing like God did, but we take what God has done and steward it in such a way that we can decree a creative force into the heavens and the earth.

We can also create gardens like Eden, filled with fruit and abundance—gardens in the natural realm and the spirit realm. We can plant words filled with life—words that when believed, decreed, and acted upon become the very thing they describe. Word seeds have the innate ability to become what they are describing. They are seeds releasing their inner codes to reproduce in the soil in which they are planted.

What possibilities has God given to man? What opportunities has He given us when we understand the principle that words are seeds? Plant words of life. Plant them in the heavens. Plant them on the earth. Plant them in your life, business, and children. Plant purpose filled seeds.

Words are very powerful. They effect change. They loose power. They release potential. They instruct. They release strategies that can be acted upon. God shows from the very beginning the vital importance and power of words. Nothing activates the Kingdom of God and the angel armies like the Word of God. Holy Spirit hovers until He hears the Word of God. God's Word activates His power and Kingdom resources.

Psalm 103:20 says that *angels hearken* to the voice of God's Word. The entire universe is made to respond to the voice of God's Word. The heavens and the earth are made to respond to the powerful voice of His Word. Amazingly, human beings made in His image and in His likeness are carriers of that Word when they are activated at the new birth. They are "lifed" by it when they are born again.

## GOD,

*You created the heavens and the earth simply by Your word. Teach me how to do the same—Your words in my mouth carry the ability to create and construct life. Teach me the power of my words so that I can be more aware of what I say and partner with You with each word I speak.*

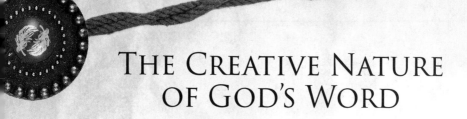

# THE CREATIVE NATURE OF GOD'S WORD

> **WE DECREE** God's Word, released through His church, sparks creativity and breakthrough.

God's Word also opens creative spheres, releasing creativity and creative abilities. Genesis 1:2 (NKJV) says, *"The earth was without form, and void; and darkness was upon the face of the deep. And the Spirit of God was hovering over the face of the waters."* The earth was without shape, in utter chaos, and it was nonproductive. It was a barren place until God's Word came forth. Notice that the condition of the heavens and the earth were dependent on the Word of God. Its productivity was dependent on the Word of God, and it still is to this day. The answer to chaos, disorder, barrenness, and darkness is the declared Word of God. The seeds of change are in the Word itself.

Philippians 2:13 (KJV) shouts this grace-filled truth: *"For it is God which worketh in you to will and to do of his good pleasure."* J.B. Rotherham's translation says, *"For it is, God, who energiseth within you, both the desiring and the energising, in behalf of his good pleasure."*

God's seed in you energizes you to create God's will by decreeing His Word. His seed becomes a creative force in the heavens and the earth when decreed by those who have His DNA, His spora. It is His plan that when His heirs open their mouth, creative spheres will open. Power to change things and bring order out of chaos will be released. Your spirit has been seeded with the DNA and nature of the living God.

God wants to energize His creative nature in you. You have been redeemed and restored to create with word seeds. Your words can create openings for God's purpose upon the earth and His will in the nations.

Your words plant the heavens with divine principles and create an environment for them to exist on the earth. The dominion mandate is not some phantom mandate that God has forgotten about. It is an eternal principle. It is expected that God's redeemed ones will rule, reign, and exercise dominion in Jesus' name. It is Godhead approved. It has His Kingdom and angel armies backing it.

We can seed the heavens with the words of God, creating change and releasing His power. We can extend His rule on the earth by planting the heavens with energized, activated words.

Those who are born-again ones, who have had God's seed sown into them, can now declare words that are seeds just like He did. It's a part of who we are. It's a part of the newborn nature God passed on. Our words spoken in faith in Christ's name become seeds that produce after their kind. Our words in His name are anointed to come to pass. We are to rule with them.

### JESUS,

*I long to seed the heavens and the earth with the words of God. I want to see Your Kingdom planted in the earth by the words that I speak. Teach me how, wonderful Jesus. Teach me how to harness the power of Your word in my mouth to see the earth saturated with Your promises and decrees.*

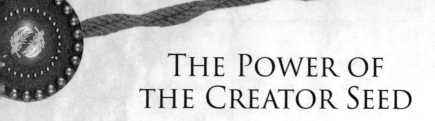

# THE POWER OF
# THE CREATOR SEED

| **WE DECREE** creative forces begin
to flow as we proclaim God's Word. |

In Isaiah 55, God tells us that His declared Word becomes creative. This now starts to get very interesting. Just as God created with His words, saying *"be"* and it was, so you and I, His legitimate seeds on the earth, are restored in purpose and identity to create with our words. Our words, in alignment with God's Word when declared in faith, become creative seeds that grow and produce after their kind. Our words become creative when they are in agreement with God's Word and in alignment with Holy Spirit and His revelation to us. They open creative spheres in a region. Think about it—how could God's creative seed literally be placed in you and you not be creative in nature? The Creator seed is in us; it is our nature to be creative with our words.

> *It is the same with my word. I send it out, and it always produces fruit. It will accomplish all I want it to, and it will prosper everywhere I send it* (Isaiah 55:11 NLT).

*It shall accomplish* is one word in the Hebrew text and it's the word *asah,* meaning "to yield out of oneself" (Strong, H6213). That's what God does—He brings out of Himself. He creates from within Himself with His words.

The entire universe came out of God. All of creation came out of God. His words framed it. His words decreed it and described it and it produced its kind. All visible, material things were decreed by God to be. They all came out of Him as He decreed His words as seeds. Of course, if the whole universe came out of God then most certainly

He can create whatever we need. How hard can that be? Our God can create any word that He speaks. No word of His is empty. When we decree God's Word, creative forces begin to flow. Even if what is needed doesn't exist, God's Word can create it.

The word *asah* also means "to become, to come to pass, to yield, or to bear" (Strong, H6213). *Asah* draws a picture of a fruit tree—it will yield whatever kind it is. The seed contains the tree that will grow from it. The fruit is also in the seed and it becomes what it is. *Asah* is also the word for *execute* or *furnish*. God's Word is furnished with power to execute and to bring that word to pass.

God's Word, when decreed by His seed in alignment with His will, becomes what it is. God says it will prosper in the thing for which He sent it. *Prosper* is the Hebrew word *tsaleach,* and it means "to push forward, to break out, to be good, to be successful, or to be profitable" (Strong, H6743). God's Word decreed becomes profitable." It breaks out of confinement. That's the way soil is pictured in the Scriptures. Soil is a confinement for the seed, but the seed breaks out of confinement to produce what it is. Word seeds break through blockages in the heavens and the earth and they are made good. They are successful. They yield and release creative abilities.

## HOLY SPIRIT,

*You are Creator God. And as Your child, I can release creative power with the words that I speak. When Your Word is decreed, it carries with it divine potential for breaking down strongholds and releasing supernatural breakthrough. Please fill my mouth with Your Word today!*

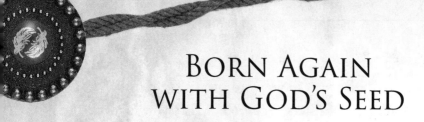

# Born Again with God's Seed

*Now that you've cleaned up your lives by following the truth, love one another as if your lives depended on it. Your new life is not like your old life. Your old birth came from mortal sperm; your new birth comes from God's living Word* (1 Peter 1:22-23 MSG).

A life conceived by God Himself opens up an area of potential and purpose that is so vast, it is mind boggling. The apostle Peter also describes God's Word as His seed. He takes us back to the very beginning to show us one of the most spectacular revelations man is ever going to receive. This incredible truth reveals God's fathering heart, yet few ever ponder it. Peter says the moment you received Jesus Christ as your Lord and Savior, God sowed His Spirit and His Word into your heart like a seed. You were born again by the incorruptible seed of the Word of God—not through corruptible seed but by the Holy Spirit and God's incorruptible Word sown into you or planted into you.

This takes Christianity and being born again to levels few have dared to ponder, let alone live out. When our minds are renewed to this truth and we understand who we really are, it activates a royal priesthood mentality.

You were born anew of incorruptible seed through the Word of God. The Greek word for *seed* is *spora,* and it's filled with new identity, new purpose, and new destiny" (Strong, G4701). It also reveals the love of God for a son or a daughter, and it explains His combined affection and care for His new "born-again" ones. It's a love that is real, pure, and constant. A love that caused the apostle John to exclaim in First John 3:1 (MSG), *"What marvelous love the Father has extended to us! Just look at it—we're called children of God! That's who we really are. But that's also why the world doesn't recognize us or take us seriously, because it has no idea who he is or what he's up to."*

Seed (*spora*) means "parenting seed, fertilized seed, or activated seed containing genetic markers, codes, or traits." It means "hereditary qualities and potentialities that are transmitted to offspring." A fertilized seed contains the parents' genetic markers. A parenting seed holds genetic codes and also generational markers.

The Holy Spirit conveys an incredible truth through the apostles about being born again. The moment you received Jesus as your Lord, God sowed His Spirit and His Word into your heart and you were born again by the incorruptible seed (*spora*) of God's Word. His parenting seed was sown into you and fertilized in your spirit. It was activated, germinated, and "lifed." Qualities and potentialities from God were transmitted to you, His offspring, much like how the seed in Mary's womb was fertilized, allowing Jesus to be supernaturally born of a virgin. You were born again—this time not through corruptible seed but by the Holy Spirit and God's incorruptible Word sown into you.

New Testament teaching is clear, and it's affirming that the parenting seed of God is sown into you at the new birth. You have God-markers in you, literally! They are planted in the core of who you are. You are born of God.

## HOLY SPIRIT,

*Thank You that I have been born again by Your seed! You have made me a new creation by the sacrifice of Jesus and I carry Your DNA. Renew my mind to this truth and let my spirit come awake to the royal priesthood mentality that You have planted inside of me.*

# DECREEING LIKE OUR FATHER

> **WE DECREE** the church is awakening!
> The sons and daughters of God are declaring
> and planting His Word into the earth.

We have to understand the power in our decrees of God's Word. Our decrees, just like Jesus Christ's decrees (our identical heir), can become creative forces that break openings in the heavens or the earth for God's purpose and His plan to produce.

We have this promise: when we stand in faith and decree what God says; when we refuse to back off; when we refuse to abandon that word seed; when we water the seed with our faith, our prayers, our praise, our confession, and our steadfast trust, the seed will produce after its kind. It becomes what it is or what it describes. Never give up on a seed you plant. Never give up on God's Word. Never. Don't negate it. We are supposed to make decrees that break loose hell's grip. We can bring forth God's promises in fullness upon the earth. As God's sons and daughters, we ought to walk this planet expecting to reap God's abundant life that His Word describes to us.

We should expect deliverance, freedom, prosperity, harvest, miracles, healings, signs, wonders, favor, strength, restoration, satisfaction, fullness, preservation, ways provided for us, help provided for us, abundance to come our way, rest for our souls, and wisdom for answers. Why? It is the seed that is in you. It's the nature of God. Remember, God's *spora* is in you. Expect the parenting seed of your Father to produce His nature. Expect His Word to produce His life everywhere.

Expect bountiful gardens to come up all around you to feed and prosper your life. Words are seeds. They grow and they become after their kind.

It is time for us to be who we really are. The world is crying out for the manifestation of the sons and daughters of God. It's time to recognize that we have God's traits passed on to us. We are heirs with authority delegated to us to be a ruling species of beings. Father's DNA is in us.

My earthly father and mother passed on genetics that can still be seen in me today. But my spirit has God's DNA in it. I am God's son—I really am! *Son* is not just some word that sounds really nice. I am here as His offspring to decree His words of life, power, and change—words that produce after their kind. Words that plant the heavens and the earth with God's Word. Word seeds that become what God says. I am here to follow the ways of my Father who has passed them on to me. It is in my spirit. It has been fertilized, germinated, and activated inside of me.

It's time we use our God-given rights as heirs of Christ to decree words that seed change everywhere. Word seed decrees that disciple a nation. Word seed decrees that declare God's power, scatter darkness, and bring order out of chaos just like His Word did in the beginning. Just like Dad did. Holy Spirit hovers until He hears God's seed declared, God's Word voiced. He's hovering today over a nation and the world, waiting for the sons and daughters of God to become the voice of God on this planet and declare His Word and not back down. It's in us to do it.

### LORD JESUS,

*I pray today for Your church to awaken to her God-given right as heirs of Christ. I pray that Your Holy Spirit would anoint her afresh to flow in her rightful authority so that Your name would be held in high honor. May Your church declare Your Word with passion and boldness and see Your Kingdom established on earth as it is in Heaven.*

# WORDS THAT YIELD HARVEST

> **I DECREE** God's word, in my mouth,
> will plant the heavens and the earth
> and I will see an abundant harvest.

*And I have put My words in your mouth; I have covered you
with the shadow of My hand, that I may plant the heavens,
lay the foundations of the earth, and say to Zion, "You are
My people"* (Isaiah 51:16 NKJV).

In this verse in Isaiah, God talks about words sounding forth from
the mouths of His sons and daughters, His heirs, into the realm of the
heavens or the earth. This again emphasizes that words are seeds—
word seed decrees. This also includes prayer because prayers are words
of communication seeded into the heavens and into the earth. Prayer
is speech to God making a request, but it is also, at times, a decree of
God's promises. Prayers express confidence in God's answering abilities,
or they may ask for divine intervention into a situation.

From the very beginning, God's original intent was for His sons and
daughters, His heirs, to open their mouths and declare His words into
the earth. He has put His Word in your mouth so that He may plant it
in the heavens and the earth. The word for *plant* is the Hebrew word
*nata,* and it means "to plant, to fix, or to set in place" (Strong, H5193).
God Himself was the original Gardener, and we have inherited that job
from Him as His heirs.

The entire universe is made to hearken to the voice of God's Word.
Heaven and earth are made to respond to the voice of God's Word. Angel
armies are made to respond to the voice of God's Word. Amazingly,

human beings, made in God's image and likeness, are also carriers of God's voice when they are activated at the new birth. As His seed on the earth, we are to open our mouths and plant the heavens and the earth with God's Word.

We are to declare the words of God into the heavens and the earth, mankind, nations, government, congregations, and people everywhere to set in place foundations for stable government and society. We are to be stewards of what God said was to be. If the foundations are not set according to God's Word, then at some point that society is going to crumble under the weight of iniquitous roots. Jesus said that such a house will not be built upon rock; it will be built upon sand, and when the storm comes it is going to fall (see Matt. 7:26).

The Body of Christ is to open their mouths and plant God's Word into the earth. "I have put My words in your mouth that I might plant the heavens and the earth." Words are the seeds we plant with.

### JESUS,

*Your words still carry the greatest hope for humanity. Your words still create life and bring transformational change. Show me today how to declare Your Word into the culture around me. Fill my mouth with Your promises and give me wisdom as to how to plant Your Word with intentionality and courage.*

# THE REALITY OF THE KING'S KINGDOM

> **WE DECREE** Kingdom, come to our region.
> Kingdom of God, come and reign over this territory.

As sons and daughters of God, we are commanded to forbid or to permit things on earth. God's original intent for His people is to reign with Him and exercise dominion, declaring God's Word into the nations. God's purpose for the church is for it to be involved in government. It is vitally important to see the church in context with Jesus Himself. That context is a King and His Kingdom.

Understand, please, that Jesus does not talk about His church first. He establishes His Kingdom first. He does that for nearly three years, and then at the very end of His ministry He mentions the church. You would think He would start off talking about His church, but He doesn't.

Jesus came to start a Kingdom that Isaiah said would have no end. You cannot understand what real church is until you understand Kingdom. The church is a part of His Kingdom.

The answer to all the chaos and confusion in our world today is the church rising up to be what Christ says the church is to be. It is abundantly clear to anyone who will take an honest look at Scripture that Jesus came to start a Kingdom. He came to build a spiritual Kingdom that would represent Him on the earth, a spiritual Kingdom that would visibly affect the earth.

When you think about a spiritual Kingdom, do not think *unreal*—think *real but unseen*. For example, while you can't see Heaven right now, decisions made in Heaven can and do affect things on the earth.

Christ's Kingdom is a spiritual Kingdom that does visibly affect the world, even though it's invisible to the natural eye. It is a real Kingdom.

Jesus Christ came teaching the reality of the Kingdom because He wanted this truth to be the worldview of His sons and daughters. If we don't understand this, Christianity does not work as originally intended, at least not to its fullest extent. The dominion mandate and the great commission to go into all the world and disciple nations will not happen without a Kingdom worldview.

Jesus did not come to start a Kingdom that would be dormant for 2,000 years. That would make no sense. He expects His Kingdom to rule and reign with Him on this earth right now. Through prayer decrees and planting God's word seeds, He expects His joint heirs to keep good foundations maintained upon the earth so that government can be built on a solid social structure. He expects them to, in His name, forbid some things and permit some things. He expects His influence to enter into a culture and change that culture through His born-again ones teaching exactly what He says. He expects His church to act like it's supposed to act and to work for what His Word says must be accomplished.

In chapter 6 of Matthew, He preaches on prayer, saying, *"In this manner, therefore, pray: Our Father in heaven, hallowed be Your name. Your kingdom come. Your will be done on earth as it is in heaven"* (Matthew 6:9-10 NKJV). The Greek speaks that in a declarative way. In other words, He said, "Kingdom, come." That's what we are to declare.

## LORD JESUS,

*Your Kingdom, come! Your Kingdom come, now! In the midst of a culture searching for answers, may Your church rise up with boldness to declare Your powerful Word. Give us Your eyes and ears for our society, teaching us what to declare and when. May Your Kingdom be established now, with each word that we speak.*

# THE AUTHORITY
# OF THE EKKLESIA

> **WE DECREE** the ekklesia of the Kingdom of
> God is rising up to take her place, influencing
> culture and bringing Kingdom change.

The picture of a kingdom that grows and prospers on the earth is
strengthened by the word Jesus chose to refer to His church. After
three years of teaching the Kingdom, He used a political, judicial,
and governmental word to introduce His church into the earth. That
astonishes a lot of people. But remember, God wants His sons and His
daughters reigning with Him. We are made in His image and He is a
ruler, a governor, and a King, so the nature to govern is planted into our
being the day that we are born again. It's a part of our spiritual DNA.

The word Jesus uses for *church* emphatically reflects that. That word
is *ekklesia,* and it is translated *church* 113 times in the New Testament
(Strong, G1577). Jesus, the disciples, and the apostles used *ekklesia* to
describe the church. It is not a religious word. It is not even a sacred word,
and in the Bible it never denotes a building or a specific place of worship.

Christ never said, "I will build My synagogue or temple, and the
gates of hell will not prevail against its walls." He said, "I will build My
ekklesia, and the gates of hell will not prevail against them." Knowing
who Jesus is and His brilliance, we have to conclude that He did not use
this word accidentally to describe His church.

We need to understand the kind of authority an ekklesia held in
order to fully grasp what Jesus meant when He used the word. "When
the Greek city-states found their governments had become too corrupt
and oppressive, they would call for an ekklesia, an assembly outside the
civil authority of the city. If enough people came out and refused to

accept the existing centralized civil authority, that government would collapse." Due to the ekklesia's authority, civil leaders could be replaced to ensure the ekklesia's rule was enforced. Wow. That's pretty strong authority. Remember, Jesus said His ekklesia would forbid some things and permit some things. There are some people we should forbid from holding office. There are others we should permit.

The Romans, who were the governing power when Christ made the statement in Matthew 16:18, also had ekklesias. Don't think Jesus didn't know it. He knew it very well. When Rome would conquer a territory they would send in a group of administrators, legislators, or regulators of culture. The idea was to make that province look like Rome, reform it to be a little Rome, and make it compatible with Roman rule. They called that governing council the ekklesia.

Now we have a more complete context for what Jesus is saying. We see what *ekklesia* meant at the time, and we see that the first mention of church is within the context of the Kingdom of God. So the contextual definition is this: "The Kingdom of God's governing, ruling body is the ekklesia, established by King Jesus to look after His Kingdom on earth." We have to get that. The ruling Kingdom is not for a future time in Heaven because it won't be necessary there.

Apostle Joseph Mattera writes that by using the word ekklesia, "Jesus called His followers the new congress of His kingdom." That's the best definition I've seen yet. Jesus says believers are to come together and they are to rule with Him in His name on the earth.

### JESUS,

*You chose to call Your church, ekklesia, for good reason. Help us be Your ekklesia, making earth look like Heaven with each passing day. Lead us to establish Your Kingdom with our words and actions, bringing Heaven's reality into our homes, cities, and nations. We long to rule with You now. We long to be Your ekklesia.*

# RULING AND REIGNING

> **WE DECREE** the church was created
> to rule and reign alongside King Jesus.

The cultural mandate of the Scriptures is that the church is called to be the moral center of the culture and the backbone of its laws by influencing every discipline and jurisdiction with a biblical worldview. It's time we were about the business of doing it and quit apologizing for it. It's time to be what Christ Jesus says we are—an ekklesia raising our hands to affect public policy, judge corruption, pass and enforce legislation that lines up with God's Word, shape the culture, speak against idolatry and vain philosophies, and speak against judges who legislate unrighteousness. We have been authorized in Jesus' name. We have been called to that purpose. I know that we will never have a utopia upon this planet until Jesus comes back. But we can affect the world and its governments, and we are expected to.

By using the word *ekklesia* Jesus was clearly saying, "Church, get involved and shape your culture. If it is wrong, don't hide. Raise your hand. Be vocal. Be public and forbid it. Rebuke things in My name. Forbid some things in My name and permit what is biblical. Affect public policy. Make sure you have the final say. Make the final choice. Get involved in the laws of your land. Get involved in matters of war and treaties. Speak up against corruption. Don't be passive and say nothing. If it's corrupt, say so. Vote it gone. Rule against it in My name. Only back those in any kind of official capacity who will obey My Word."

"Ekklesia, church, speak up against adultery in your capital, your gates. Rule against ridiculous philosophies that are coming out of your capitals and ideas or philosophies that justify sin and pollute the culture. Speak up and raise your hand. Vote and rule against it. You're My legislative body on the planet. You're My congress. Regulate the laws of your land. Regulate the culture you are going to live in. Say no to social corruption. Transform your territories. Shape them to look like a little bit of Heaven on earth. Shape the culture you are living in. Decide societal issues. Decide the economy. Decide tax issues, and only back those who honor the Word of God."

We have wrongly bought the idea that we are to stay out of politics, legislation, and cultural decisions when, in fact, the very word for *church* in Scripture is a political word—a ruling body, a governing body, a legislative body. It is a congress, and make no mistake—Jesus knew exactly what that was.

The church is to be Christ's ruling body on the earth. Remember from Romans 8:17 (NKJV), we are *"heirs of God, and joint-heirs with Christ."* We are identical heirs with Christ right now, and in His name we are to rule on the earth. Yes, we are going to rule with Him through eternity, but we need to reign with Him now as well. We should not dispensationalize it away into the future.

## LORD JESUS,

*As Your sons and daughters, You have given us the mandate to affect the culture around us. You have called us to implement change in society by our influence and in partnership with Your Spirit. Anoint us today to stand for truth and morality, ruling and reigning with You.*

# OPERATING IN OUR RIGHTFUL AUTHORITY

> **WE DECREE** the remnant Bride carries herself
> with authority, both in word and in action.

If we are going to plant the heavens and lay God's Word into our culture's foundations, we must learn, practice, and activate authority language. The King's seed that is sown into us, the King's DNA that has been transmitted into our spirit at the new birth, needs to manifest inside of us. We need to become who and what we really are. We are under the Lordship of King Jesus, forgiven, re-imaged, and born again into His family. We truly are in the King's lineage. We are heirs of God and we are joint heirs with Christ. We are a part of the Kingdom of Almighty God and are expected to reign with Him right now.

As part of His family, we need to engage in releasing words of power, might, and dominion. If we are going to see things change, we must restore kingly speech and authority language to the Body of Christ. It's time to decree our Kingdom authority, to rise up and rule in this life as intended. It's time to fill and occupy the earth, subduing it and exercising dominion. We should be advancing into positions of authority as the Holy Spirit leads.

We are not here to be ruled by unrighteousness. That makes no sense. Why would God put us here to be ruled by unrighteousness? We have been legally established as governors, ruling ones given authority by our God. We are heirs now, and we are to declare the uncompromised Word of King Jesus on the earth. We are not to compromise it. We are not to make it politically correct. We are to say what He says.

Jesus talked as though He was authorized. He used His words to influence. The words of our King were forceful. He spoke like a potentate. He spoke like a magistrate who knew His jurisdiction. He spoke with power. His words were sure and spoken with might.

In Luke 4:36 (NKJV) it says, *"Then they were all amazed and spoke among themselves, saying, 'What a word this is! For with authority and power He commands the unclean spirits, and they come out.'"*

Our King spoke against demon powers and ruled over them. He gave commands to demons. He didn't take commands. He activated His authority with His words, and like a master magistrate He told devils to go and they did. Shouldn't we do likewise? Shouldn't His church do likewise? Shouldn't His heirs' speech drip with authority? Are we not supposed to represent Him? Aren't we to do what He did?

Kings talk differently. Their speech resonates with authority. They carry themselves with authority. It's time for a remnant Bride to begin to carry herself with authority, knowing that a yes on earth is a yes in Heaven and a no on earth is a no in Heaven. Knowing that Heaven, Holy Spirit, and angel armies are backing it up.

## HOLY SPIRIT,

*I pray today for your remnant Bride to be filled with the fire of Your presence. Fill our mouths with the words of Your heart. Restore kingly speech to Your church, so that our words may bring change and transformation into the lives around us. Thank You that as we decree Your words, angels are backing us up.*

# TALKING LIKE JESUS

| **WE DECREE** the Kingdom of Heaven is here, now. |

In Mark 13:31 (KJV), Jesus said, "*Heaven and earth shall pass away: but my words shall not pass away.*" He said, "My words are different. They are powerful and energized with authority to produce. My words cause dynamic effects. I use my words to rule and reign in this life on the earth. You're joint heirs with Me; you do the same thing"

Jesus spoke spirit words that are alive and powerful, words quickened by the Holy Spirit. To represent our King and our Kingdom, we must learn to speak kingly language. We have to speak strong, forceful, confident words that are powerful and effective. We cannot give an uncertain sound and reign with Him on the earth. We've got to speak words that rulers and magistrates speak. Knowing our authority, it's time to speak with authority. We must plant God's words into the heavens and the earth. They will activate and germinate. They will produce after their kind. They will produce what they are.

To represent Jesus, we must talk like Him. We are to release commanding words of power and authority against demon powers that rise against us. Knowing who we are, we are to exercise Kingdom jurisdiction in our region. We are to live, move, act, and talk like kings under King Jesus. We're to speak words in His name that are alive, active, and powerful. They are words based upon God's Word, His covenant, His laws, and His principles. We're to activate our authority with our words—the world needs it badly right now.

Sadly, we have embraced the language of sheep rather than the language of kings. Yes, like sheep we follow our great Shepherd Jesus, listening for His voice. We go where He leads. We follow no one else and submit to no one else. But our language is to be the language of kings as we reign with Him like kings and priests. It's time we discern what the Spirit of God is really saying. We do not bow sheepishly to an ungodly world. We do not say "baaaa" to demons. We say, "Go in the name of Jesus Christ." We say, "Be bound by superior forces of the Kingdom of Almighty God in Jesus' name." We say, "We will decide what is done on earth, not you." We do not sheepishly bow to the gates of hell.

We cannot represent a King who spoke with power with wimpy, reticent words from doubtful minds. We cannot represent Him with negative statements from intimidated thinking. We cannot stand in the face of demons from hell and speak quiet, shy words of compromise. We cannot sheepishly run from the gates or the authorities of hell.

We cannot gaze silently and then just slink away in spineless apprehension like slaves rather than kings. We can't speak dispirited, lifeless words of human doctrine. We can't declare His doctrine in power and ours in impotence. He cannot speak living words of faith and we speak dead words of doubt. We cannot feebly declare the Kingdom of Heaven is here. No—if it's here, we need to declare it with power and authority language.

### HOLY SPIRIT,

*I ask today for a fresh touch from You. I need Your Spirit to represent Your Kingdom well. I long to embrace the language of King Jesus, my mouth filled with His words. I want my life to declare with power and authority that the Kingdom of Heaven is here, now!*

# SPEAKING THE KING'S LANGUAGE

> **WE DECREE** the King's voice is filling the lips of the ekklesia.

Kings speak with authority. To be kings and priests of His household who rule and reign with Him in this life, we are going to have to do it with some boldness. We must declare the Word of God with authority. The early church understood this, and we need to understand it also. The prophets and apostles in the Book of Acts operated in very bold authority. They spoke the king's language.

God confirmed their bold faith commands with signs, wonders, and miracles. He gave them harvest after harvest after harvest until harvests were no longer added to them—they were multiplied to them. Their influence turned the world upside down. Today's church is being reintroduced to a revelation that is indeed revolutionary.

The ekklesia is going to rise up and become the King's voice upon this earth again. The King's voice is going to fill their lips. The church is rising from the ash heaps of religious bondage. It is rising from the desolation of pharisaical laws. His ekklesia is rising in spite of critical spirits designed to muzzle God's people. It is rising in spite of political pressure and even societal pressure to keep silent. His born-again ones are rising in spite of politically correct language that is intolerant and even despises those who will stand for something.

The King's kids in His church are starting to find their voice. The saints are rising to a new level of authority because Christ the King will have a strong, clear, powerful, bold voice on the earth. He will be represented accurately and well.

We need to pray with authority language. We need to speak with authority language. We need to decree our faith with authority language. We need to say what God says with authority language.

It is time to release authority language into your atmosphere. Until it's decreed, the seed is dormant. It's time to plant the heavens. It's time to plant the earth. It's time to decree what God says. What God says matters and it will work. God is on our side. He said, "A *no* on earth is a *no* in Heaven if you will boldly say it in My name, and a *yes* on earth is a *yes* in Heaven. What do you want, a *yes* or a *no*? I am delegating it to you."

Exercise your God-given authority and begin decreeing today, "Father, because we are joint heirs with Jesus, in His name we rise to plant the heavens and the earth with faith decrees aligned with Your Word."

Lord, let the church, the ekklesia, the sons and daughters, the born-again ones rise to plant the heavens and the earth with Your words. We will continue to do so, ruling and reigning as You purposed, refusing to allow hell's kingdom to reign over us. We rise today to face and bind principalities, powers, mights, and dominions. We will not say "baaaa" to them. We will not sheepishly stand for You. We decree Your Kingdom with power, come and reign through Your church in the name of Jesus Christ. We declare it. Amen.

JESUS,

*I bless Your ekklesia today to rise and be filled with the King's language. I bless Your church to decree with power and zeal that Your Kingdom is coming, now, in Jesus' name. Let Your Spirit rest upon us, let your angels minister to us and may we bring You glory with each word we speak.*

# THE UNVEILING

| **WE DECREE** it is time for the unveiling. |

I want to share a prophetic word the Lord recently gave me:

Holy Spirit says to remnant warriors—it is time for the unveiling. The great season has now come and the curtain is being drawn and the world will now see the scintillating Kingdom of King Jesus rising from the ashes of a beguiled world. See it, says the Lord. See its radiant glory. It's intensifying, accelerating, and revealing your King as the supreme commander of Heaven and of earth.

It's time for the reveal of the supernatural into the natural, says the Lord. There will now be seen a spiritual Kingdom that visibly affects the world. It will visibly affect earthly kingdoms. It will visibly affect world leaders. It will visibly affect governments. It will visibly affect the marketplace, the education system, and the media. Like leaven, the mighty Kingdom of God and His Christ will penetrate the earth as never before.

No more delay, says Heaven. Darkness will now be penetrated and dispelled by glorious light. Deception will be dispelled by glorious truth. Iniquity will be uprooted by glorious power. Demon thrones will be toppled by glorious authority, dominating authority, supreme authority, ruling, and reigning authority. Bondage will be broken by glorious liberty. Curses will now be reversed by glorious blessings. Principalities and powers, mights and dominions will be toppled by the superior forces of My Kingdom, says the Lord of Hosts.

My kingdom is rising, and it will now be revealed in new ways and in new displays. It cannot be stopped. It cannot be hindered. It cannot be compromised. My spiritual kingdom will visibly affect this world. It will rise. It will rule, and it will reign with wisdom and with awesome power. It has been, it is, and it will be increasing upon the earth with jealous aggression and with striking power from Heaven flashing down to your planet, says the Lord. Yes, a Kingdom that has no end and no equal will now be revealed as promised.

The surge of Heaven has now begun. The world has never seen the like; a functioning spiritual Kingdom that's at hand. Yes. You can touch it. Yes, it is among you—a Kingdom that is coming. It keeps coming and coming and coming, and it is coming until an even greater reveal—My coming in the clouds of glory. For you are entering into the season of the mighty King who prevails, a King who will make His stand. His Kingdom is growing and His Kingdom will prevail. And the prevailing anointing of Jesus will now be seen upon His remnant people.

As in His first ekklesia, so mightily grew the Word and it prevailed, so it will be in your times. Anointing to prevail is now being poured out upon you. You will prevail. The King's Word on your lips will prevail mightily. Speak on the King's behalf. Speak His Word from your lips. Speak as ambassadors in His Kingdom; and as you speak, you will grow. And as you speak, you will prevail...

## HOLY SPIRIT,

*Thank You that Your words give us new insight and revelation for the days ahead. Thank You that that earth has never seen what You are about to pour out. Thank You that Your Kingdom is once again being revealed in new ways and King Jesus will make His stand. Anoint us to prevail!*

# DESTINED TO WIN

| **WE DECREE** the Lord will have His harvest! |

The Lord continued with the prophetic word...

Increase is increasing. Bounty is abounding; power is compounding. Promises believed for will grow, and they will prevail to fullness before your eyes. Prophetic words will prevail to fullness. My Word will not return void. Supernatural deliverance will now prevail to fullness. Healings and miracles will now prevail to fullness. Dreams and visions will now prevail to fullness. Decrees of your faith will now prevail to fullness. Cries of your heart will prevail to fullness. It is "yes" and it is "amened" by Heaven. My church will prevail, says the Lord. The gates of hell will not prevail. The authority of hell cannot prevail. It is written, and it cannot be reversed. It is the immutable decree of your King, so act in accordant confidence.

Lucifer is not omnipresent, but I am. Lucifer is not omniscient, but I am. Lucifer is not omnipotent, but I am. Lucifer's kingdom is not unshakable, but Mine is. Act in accordant confidence. And I will now lead the greatest move of My Kingdom in all of history. Holy Spirit is now activating My coalition.

I will have My harvest. I will have an allied partnership with Me—remnant champions who will know I am God with them. They will know I have allied Myself and My Kingdom with them. It will be seen. I am God with them everywhere. I am wisdom and knowledge with them everywhere. I'm the all-powerful one with them everywhere. I'm the prevailing one with them everywhere. They will prevail everywhere; for the coalition forces of My Kingdom have now been called to the battle line. The multiplied strength of My allies joined together for My Kingdom's cause has never been stronger. My angel armies, My remnant warriors, My Holy Spirit, My Father, and all of Heaven have allied with Me and My Kingdom. Fight one of us, you fight us all.

Covenants are now established. Treaties have been signed with My blood. Alignments have initiated assignments, and My allied coalition is strong and enduring. No, hell cannot prevail. My church will prevail. My remnant will prevail; for yes, My Kingdom has been attacked. And yes, My remnant has been pressed in great battle, but know that a mighty Kingdom is allied with you. Know that the King of kings is allied with you. Know that Holy Spirit and His angel armies are allied with you. Know that Almighty God and all of Heaven is allied with you. You will not fight this battle alone. Allies are at hand. Allies are among you. Allies are rushing to the battlefront with you.

My Kingdom, My power, and My anointing to prevail is upon you. You will win against hell's opposing forces. Hell cannot stop you, so arise with My Kingdom and, with great confidence, begin to rule and begin to reign with Me with great boldness, understanding My coalition is behind you. Go and influence earth as My ambassadors. Go and stand for My truth. Go and declare My Word without compromise. Go and make a determined stand for My cause. Go, it is part of My coalition. Rule in the midst of your enemies, says the Lord. Go and in His name prevail.

## LORD JESUS,

*You are the rightful King! And as Your church we receive Your anointing to prevail in this hour, rising with Your Kingdom to rule and reign alongside of You. No tactic of the enemy will win. You, King Jesus, are the Victorious One and You will have your harvest!*

# Doers of the Word

> **WE DECREE** a reversal of the
> prescription of hell for this nation.

Prayer is decreeing a purpose that God can make so. Very few these days understand that the church is here to rule and reign with Christ *right now.*

Few know and understand this because it's been dispensationalized by many into something that's in the future somewhere, not to be done right now. Very few understand the true purpose of God's sons and daughters or the church that Jesus came to establish. We need to be reminded of some things because we can change and disciple a nation. If we do, our personal lives are going to succeed at much higher levels.

We are in a season when clearly we need to *do* the Word of God. The world is divided and crumbling because the church and millions of Christians are not doing their assignment. The world that most of us knew growing up is coming apart at the seams because much of the church has not been doing what God says. We have to be doers of the Word of God. Allow the Holy Spirit to activate this in you.

We need to pay close attention to how words are used. The word *decree* is used ten times throughout the Book of Esther. Nine times the word *decree* is a translation of the Hebrew word *dath,* but Esther's decree is a different word. It is *maamar,* and it is used only one time.

*Dath,* used nine times, means "an edict, a statute, a law, a command, a prescription, or legislation" (Strong, H1881). *Maamar* means "something spoken with authority." It refers to king's language or a royal edict" (Strong, H3982). King's language, authority language, was given to Mordecai and Esther to reverse evil legislation, laws, and government action. Esther 8 tells us that they did use it and they did do it. Authority to decree against and change evil laws was given to them, creating a picture of what Christ did for us through the cross.

As the King's heirs on the earth, we have been restored to use authority language. We have been restored to speak with royal dominion. We have been restored to speak royal edicts for our kingdom. We have received authority in Jesus' name to stop evil prescriptions and laws and to decree God's prescriptions as His kids. We are here to decree God's statutes, laws, ways, and will. We are here to declare God's prescription for our lives, over our assignments, and for our nation. As Christ's joint heirs, we are here to reign in this life using authority language (see Rom. 8:17). *Maamar*—release words of power and authority and make kingly declarations so God can make it so.

Authority language was given to Mordecai and Esther to decree a stop to evil laws, to stop an attack against God's people. Kingly language to change a nation was given to them. I see a very strong parallel that pictures the calling of God to His people and to His church right now.

## HOLY SPIRIT,

*In Jesus' name, I partner with Heaven to cancel the prescription of hell over my nation, my family, and my life. I declare the Kingdom of God's royal edicts, statutes, laws, and ways. I decree Your prescription for our lives and our nation! Your Kingdom come and Your will be done!*

# DECREEING THE PROMISES OF GOD

| **WE DECREE** the promises of God are materializing now in Jesus' name. |

Decrees create. They can create ideas in your heart. They create things that are not seen with the natural eye. They can create changes in conditions and in the atmosphere physically, spiritually, emotionally, materially, governmentally, politically, vocationally, and provisionally. Decrees are a creative force and they release a creative force that will bless us abundantly.

In Isaiah 42:9 (KJV) God says, *"New things do I declare: before they spring forth I tell you of them."* Notice that He says, "I declare them before they spring forth. I pronounce them before they ever are." Smith and Goodspeed's translation reads, *"New things I foretell—before they spring into being, I will announce them to you."* So God says, "I announce them. I declare without negation first so that they can be seen."

God says, "If it is to be, if I have purposed it to be, I will speak it first before it ever comes to life." First comes a decree—a declared word that He will not change or negate. The Living Bible reads, *"I will prophesy again. I will tell you the future before it happens."* That's what prophecy is—foretelling something before it happens. Anyone can prophesy after something happens. God says, "I explain with My words what is to be before it ever is, and then it springs forth and materializes. It doesn't materialize until I speak it. It doesn't materialize until there's a decree." That's what Hebrews 11:1 is about—faith decreed becomes substantive. Faith-filled words materialize if you don't negate them.

The word *before* in Isaiah 42:9 is the Hebrew word *tehrem*. It is a very important word for believers and the church to understand because it means "suspended in time" or "not yet occurred" (Strong, H2962). So God says, "While its existence is suspended in time, while it has not yet occurred, I decree it."

In Genesis 22:18, God told a man named Abraham—Abram at the time—that he was going to be the heir of the world and the father of nations. Notice that this was before Abram ever had a son, and God decreed this to Abram when it was impossible for him. Abram was 99 years old and Sarah was 89 years old, well past the age to bear children. But God isn't bound to any limitations. He wasn't bothered by what Sarah and Abram looked like or their age. It didn't matter.

While having a child was suspended in time and before it occurred (*tehrem*), God prophesied it. While it looked impossible, God announced it. He declared it. He spoke authority words of faith. He created what was impossible for man with His words. You must decree words of faith first in order to create promises that are impossible where man is concerned. You must declare what seems impossible in the natural realm to see it materialized. Then it can spring forth, sprout, bud, and grow to fullness.

The promise will remain impossible, suspended in time, until it's decreed. The moment it's decreed, it becomes possible. When the promise is decreed, it is conceived—it goes past mere knowledge and becomes substance that is planted and can grow.

## LORD GOD,

*Thank You that You always see the promise fulfilled. Thank You that You speak into what seems like an impossible situation and bring life and hope. Thank You that Your word declared releases the authority of Heaven and creates promises fulfilled. I partner with faith today to believe You and what You have spoken!*

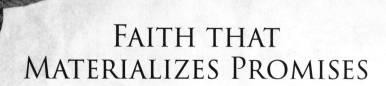

# FAITH THAT MATERIALIZES PROMISES

> **WE DECREE** promises of God,
> come here and come here now!

I often hear someone who is believing for a promise say, "But I don't see any evidence of this." Exactly! That is the point! You don't see any evidence because it is suspended in time. It doesn't exist yet. Quit looking at that. You cannot see evidence until you plant a decree. But people say, "Well, if I say that, I am lying." No—you are creating it, not lying. Don't negate it, create it.

In the beginning, God didn't see trees and then tell us about trees. There were no trees. While they were suspended in time, He said *"be"* and they sprang forth. True faith calls it *done* in Jesus' name, and then the promises can sprout, bud, and grow to fullness. What seems impossible becomes possible, ready to be watered by our faith and brought to fullness.

Romans 4:17 (KJV) reads, *"God...calleth those things which be not as though they were."* The New English Translation reads, *"God who makes the dead alive and summons the things that do not yet exist as though they already do."* He summons or calls to them. That is the best translation. That is what the Greek text describes—decrees summon something to come to you. Authority language summons what does not exist yet to come to you. It speaks of it as being done. The Living Bible reads, *"God... speaks of future events with as much certainty as though they were already past." Calleth* is the Greek word *kaleo* and it means "to say out loud, to bid, to call something near you, and to summon" (Strong, G2564).

The phrase *those things* is translated from one Greek word in the original text—*ousa*, meaning "to be" and "being" (Strong, G5607). But it primarily means "to come." So when you put the two together, *kaleo ousa* would mean "come here" or "come to me." Say aloud, *"Come here. Come to me. Come here now."*

In verse 17, *not* is the Greek word *me* (pronounced like "may"), and it means "no existence, nothing, and to deny" (Strong, G3361). Faith says to things that have no existence, "Come here. Come here now." Faith summons them.

We must use kingly language toward nonexistent things or things that must be changed. In Jesus' name, we are to boldly decree—to things that are suspended in time, to promises that have not been fulfilled yet, to prophecy that has not occurred yet—"Come here and manifest to me."

As believers, we need to begin to declare, "Come here and come here now." To promises that hell's kingdom may be denying you, you've got to start saying with bold authority, "Come here. Come to me, healing. Come to me, finances. Come to me, new job. Come to me. Manifest. Take on substance. Sprout, bud, and grow. I am not going to make this command negative any longer. I'm not cancelling. In Jesus' name, you come here."

Decree the promise is yours. Proclaim that the promise is yours and don't negate it. The Scriptures plainly teach that decrees come first. You have to decree before it's ever conceived. Proclaim the promise and then it materializes. It doesn't materialize until it's decreed and not negated.

## GOD,

*Today I posture my heart in faith toward You and Your promises. I remind myself of the promises You've spoken over me and agree with You, decreeing that the promises are mine in Jesus' name. Thank You for the life that Your promises infuse into my heart and my mind!*

# THE MOST VALUABLE
# WORD SEED

| **I DECREE** that God's Word is bringing fresh life to me and my faith. |

God's Word itself is possibly the most valuable source of word seed decrees that will life you and your faith. We need to learn to decree the Scriptures in such a way that they are personalized into our lives. It's a very simple thing that I have practiced for about thirty years now. I spend an hour or more doing this at least a couple times a month. It has blessed my life and helped me through some very difficult times.

I often read these passages and then personalize them. For example, most people know Psalm 23, "The Lord is my Shepherd." But when you put that in decree form it starts to transform your life and feed you in a different way. When I put it in the decree form after reading it, it sounds something like this:

King Jesus is my Shepherd and I don't want for anything. I want for nothing, and I will never want for anything because my King Jesus is my Shepherd. He makes me to lie down in places of great resources that will only feed my life. That will happen to me this day. He leads me beside the still waters. He will never lead me into troubling places. He leads me to restful places and He restores my soul. No matter what comes to deplete me, my King will be there to restore and life me afresh and anew. He will lead me in great paths today— paths of righteousness. Right ways will be before me, and I will be led down the right path; even if I walk through the valley of death, I fear no evil. I will not fear evil. I don't have to fear any kind of evil because He is always with me. I fear no evil. His rod, His staff, they are always there to comfort me. Even if I come into the presence of my enemies, I will have nothing to fear because He will spread a banquet for me. He will resource me anyway, no matter what situation I find myself in. He anoints me with fresh oil. My cup is going to run over. The anointing of the Kingdom of God is overflowing and running through my life. Goodness is following me everywhere I go. Mercy is following me everywhere I go. Favor is following me everywhere I go, and it will be that way all the days of my life. I will dwell in the house of the Lord forever because I am a part of His family. I am a son/daughter of God. I have a right to be in His house. His presence is where I live. Because I live in His presence only goodwill come my way.

That is a decree based upon the Word of God, and it is so easy to do. Just follow along and declare it, and when you do the Word will reset you for what is ahead. Your words will line up with God's Word, and when something happens you will find yourself decreeing what God says.

### LORD JESUS,

*When I consider Your words and ponder what You have said, my heart is anchored and my eyes have fresh vision. Your Word is a lamp to my feet and a light to my path. May Your words reset me for what is ahead. May my first response to any situation be to declare Your life-giving truth!*

# THE POWER OF
# OUR WORDS

**I DECREE** that my mind is set to God's Word.

*For we all stumble in many things. If anyone does not stumble in word, he is a perfect man, able also to bridle the whole body. Indeed, we put bits in horses' mouths that they may obey us, and we turn their whole body* (James 3:2-3 NKJV).

The emphasis here is on the whole body. The tongue, the speech, and the words of our mouth are compared to a horse's bit and bridle. If you have ever ridden a horse, you know that one of the ways that you control that horse is through the bit and the bridle. If you pull the rein to the left, the horse goes to the left. If you pull to the right, then it's going to go to the right. The words of our mouth are compared to the bit and bridle—we are controlled by them. We're pulled one way or the other by the words that we speak. Our words have the ability to stop us or give us free rein to move. They control the whole body. Every part of our being, James says, is controlled by the tongue and the words of our mouth.

King Solomon adds emphasis in Proverbs 18:21, saying, *"Death and life are in the power of the tongue."* The potential for life and death are both present. Your words will either bless you or curse you. They will either produce life or they will produce death. They are under the power of the tongue. *Power* is the Hebrew word *yad*. It means "in the hand of" or "under the direction of" (Strong, H3027).

Proverbs 12:6 (KJV) says, *"The mouth of the upright shall deliver them."*

Why is that? Because the mouth of an upright man speaks right words and right words are forcible. Right words are words that agree with God's Word implanted into our heart, and those words decreed in Jesus' name bring deliverance. Proverbs 12:18 (KJV) says, *"The tongue of the wise is health."* Proverbs 13:3 (NKJV) says, *"He who guards his mouth preserves his life."* Right words preserve life, destiny, prosperity, health, and vision. Proverbs 16:24 (NKJV) says, *"Pleasant words are like a honeycomb, sweetness to the soul and health to the bones."* The welfare of your entire being depends on the words of your mouth. Your words life you. Your life, health, wellbeing, and destiny are determined by your words.

Words are powerful. Words release potential. Words open up more destiny to you. Words establish vision. Do it out loud with courage. Decree these words:

> I am everything God says I am. I can do everything God says I can do. I will speak with my mouth what God says about me. I am healthy. I am righteous. I'm at peace. I am wise. I am prosperous. I'm successful. I'm an heir of God and a joint heir with Christ. I'm a conqueror. I'm a winner. I'm an overcomer. Holy Spirit lives in me. His power is at work in me. Therefore, I live my life in victory. Amen. So be it.

## HOLY SPIRIT,

*Your Words declared open up new realms of possibility, peace, life and hope. Teach me to steward what I say with wisdom, partnering with Your voice over my life and situation. Fill my mouth with Your powerful truth. I long to represent You well in word and action, releasing Your Kingdom and establishing Your Lordship.*

# SPEAKING TO MOUNTAINS

> **I DECREE** any oppressive adversity that attempts to strangle my purpose and my destiny, my future, hopes and dreams, go now in Jesus' name!

*Then Jesus said to the disciples, "Have faith in God. I tell you the truth, you can say to this mountain, 'May you be lifted up and thrown into the sea,' and it will happen. But you must really believe it will happen and have no doubt in your heart. I tell you, you can pray for anything, and if you believe that you've received it, it will be yours"* (Mark 11:22-24 NLT).

Whatever you believe and decree will happen. That's astounding. I'm glad Jesus made this statement. If He hadn't said it, we might doubt it. A part of the Godhead said it, not some pastor somewhere. Jesus said it, so God definitely meant for you to know this. This was not a slip of the tongue or a divine oops. He wants you to rule and reign with Him (see Rom. 5:17). *Mountain, go there and go there now. Hindrance, get away from me. Come here, go there.* We have authority to summon or to send away. We can send away from us what hinders our benefits from getting to us. It may take some time, it may take some spiritual warfare, it may not always be easy, but we cannot say that it is impossible.

We have looked primarily at summoning blessings to us, but sometimes there are things that have to be dispatched or sent away in the name of Jesus. We have to send some things packing. Spirit of poverty, go from me. Spirit of heaviness, go from me. Depression and hopelessness, go from me. Fear, cancer, disease, demon activity of every kind, oppressive adversity that attempts to strangle our purpose and destiny, our future, hopes and dreams, we are to exercise authority and dispatch it from us in the name of Jesus. It is subject to the word of faith in our heart being declared. Clearly, God wants us to act on our authority.

Jesus said, "Whoever shall say to the mountain." The word for *say* there is the Greek word *epo,* meaning "to speak with authority, to command, and it pictures a general or a king who stands before troops and gives a command or an order to them" (Strong, G2036). It means "to tell and to order." Jesus said that those in authority, His heirs, can command things to come or to go. They can command, tell, or give orders to mountains or to obstructions that come to hinder their lives.

*Mountain* is the Greek word *oros,* and it means "to rise, to lift up above the plain, and to rear up" (Strong, G3735). A mountain is an obstacle that rises, rears up, and blocks our pathway. It could be a sickness, disease, financial trouble, a job loss—anything. We have authority to command it to go, change, or make a correction in accordance with the Word of God—to turn and actually become good for us. Any mountain that rises up, you have authority to decree "Go" to it in Jesus' name, and you have authority to command it to begin to align with the Word of God. "Conform to the promise of God in my life. Come to me now and manifest."

## JESUS,

*Please give me Your eyes to see the mountains in my life and command them to leave in Your powerful name. Anoint me with fresh boldness to speak to any obstacle or delay and command it to make a correction in accordance with Your Word. In faith, I speak to every mountain and declare that it must conform to Your promises!*

# GROWING FAITH

> **I DECREE** that my faith has been planted
> and is growing to maturity now in Jesus' name.

There is a faith that moves mountains, but mountain moving faith often must be grown. That requires perseverance and consistency on our part. Mountains do not move by small faith; they move by great faith that is consistently grown. You move mountains by faith that is maintained, nurtured, and guarded. Faith grows to maturity and produces what is decreed. You change circumstances and situations, not by a faith that is moved by what it sees or how it feels, but by a faith that is moved by the Word of the Living God.

In 1998, I was studying Matthew 17:14-20. As I read, a valuable principle and a very freeing truth began to be revealed. I began to see faith differently than the way I had been taught as a young boy in Sunday school. For the first time, I began to see faith as a seed that could grow and meet the challenge of a mountain.

This passage revealed *growing faith* to me. I heard Holy Spirit say, "You need to grow your faith," and I began to see some things I hadn't considered before. I had to plant faith with my words aligned with God's Word so it could grow to challenge and overcome the mountain.

A man came to Jesus with his son who was in real trouble. The child kept throwing himself into the fire trying to commit suicide. You can imagine, if you were the parent of a child like that you would have to watch them all the time. This was a horrible situation. The man told Jesus he brought his son to the disciples who prayed over him, but nothing happened. So the man decided to bring his son to Jesus. We are told that Jesus rebuked the evil spirit that was tormenting this child, set him free, and he was absolutely totally healed from that moment on.

Later on the disciples came privately to Jesus and said, "Why couldn't we take care of this? Why couldn't we drive that spirit out and heal that child?" Jesus answered them, "It's because of your unbelief."

Please understand that these disciples had faith. They weren't completely faithless; they just lacked the faith it took to change this situation.

They forgot the basic tenet of apostolic doctrine—faith needs to be maintained, nurtured with God's Word, guarded against any negativity, and kept alive and growing. This is what Jesus was teaching here in this passage.

He says faith is living, alive, and growing. A seed isn't active; it's asleep. It isn't growing; it's in a state of dormancy. A seed is a potential harvest that is not activated yet. Words are what activate the seeds. You have to plant your faith with words that align with God's Word and then keep your confession of faith consistent, keep those word seed decrees free of unbelief. The DNA of the seed you plant will then sprout, bud, and grow to fullness. Plant words of faith and keep them growing. Sow words of faith that will lay a foundation for good life, and don't negate them. Plant God's Word and let it grow to move mountains.

## HOLY SPIRIT,

*I confess that my faith needs to grow. Help me plant Your Word consistently so that the mountains in my life have no choice but to move, change and align with what You have said. Remind me to nurture and steward my faith, day after day, so that what was once a seed may become a bountiful harvest.*

# MOUNTAIN MOVING FAITH

**I DECREE** this mountain is
moving because my faith is growing!

*Then He said, "To what shall we liken the kingdom of
God? Or with what parable shall we picture it? It is like
a mustard seed which, when it is sown on the ground, is
smaller than all the seeds on earth; but when it is sown, it
grows up and becomes greater than all herbs, and shoots out
large branches, so that the birds of the air may nest under its
shade"* (Mark 4:30-32 NKJV).

*Grows up* is the Greek word *anabaino,* and it means "to arise, to
spring up, or to ascend" (Strong, G305). *Ana* is the Greek word for *up*,
"to climb up, to climb higher, or ascend up." *Baino* is a word meaning
"to go or to move up higher or go to a different level." Jesus is talking
about a faith that grows up. It's a faith that is alive. It's growing, maturing, and kept that way.

Sometimes we face a situation and our faith is just too small to
handle it. We need faith to change it. What do you do? Jesus said you
grow it! You go to work on your faith and you move it up. You soak your
heart in what God says, and you keep doing that while your faith grows.
You say what God says and refuse to negate it.

If faith isn't kept alive and growing, it goes into dormancy. Uncer-
tainty comes and we find ourselves facing situations that do not change,
and we wonder why when we saw victories in our past by faith. Like
the disciples, we need to remember that faith needs to be maintained,
guarded, matured, and kept alive. Keep it healthy. As Christ's disciples,

we never mature beyond the need to water the seed with God's Word. You water it, feed it, confess it, and declare it to move it to a higher level.

In 1952, Sir Edmund Hillary attempted to climb Mt. Everest, the highest peak on earth—29,000 feet above sea level. A few weeks after the expedition failed to climb Mt. Everest, he was asked to address a group of people in England. Sir Edmund Hillary walked up to speak, and at the edge of the stage he made a fist and he pointed at a picture of Mt. Everest. He said to that picture in a very loud voice, "Mt. Everest, you beat me the first time, but I'm going to beat you the next time because you've grown all you're going to grow but I'm still growing." On May 29, 1953, one year later, Sir Edmund Hillary became the first man to ever climb Mt. Everest.

The mountain is as big as it's going to get, but you're still growing. Your faith can still grow. You can outgrow it. Move it up. *Anabaino.* Grow your faith to another level until you beat it, and then use that deeper faith. It may be turbulent, it may be dangerous, but you can grow your faith to a level that anchors you. You can grow it to move a mountain.

## LORD JESUS,

*Today I soak my heart and my mind in what You have spoken. Your words are life to me. Your words infuse me with fresh strength and courage. Your voice is my greatest anchor. And because of what You have said, I can boldly declare, "My faith is still growing!" and I have great hope.*

# THE ROLE OF A NEW TESTAMENT CHURCH

> **WE DECREE** God is building an angel-assisted New Testament church that will be able to execute the five-fold ministry and perform as soldiers in an apostolate.

Words are powerful enough to inspire movements, which is why we plant the heavens with word seed decrees. One of the greatest word seed decrees is the apostle Paul's manifesto.

> *For though we walk in the flesh, we do not war after the flesh. For the weapons of our warfare are not carnal but mighty in God for pulling down strongholds* (2 Corinthians 10:3-4 NKJV).

He says very clearly there is a war, we have weapons, and there are strongholds that we are supposed to pull down. The word for *war* is the Greek word *strateuomai,* and it means "to serve in a military campaign" (Strong, G4754). Uniquely, it is a word used only in the first-century church of Paul's day, referring to an apostolate. An apostolate, a New Testament church, is one that is actively releasing the fivefold ministry of apostles, prophets, evangelists, pastors, and teachers as listed in Ephesians 4:11. Literally, *war* means "to execute the plans and purposes of a New Testament church."

The early church considered it a privileged duty to execute and extend the strategies of Heaven in their region. It was not forced rhetoric but privileged obedience. What would happen today if millions considered it an honor to execute and extend Holy Spirit-prompted strategies to reform culture in their regions through apostolates? Like the early church, they would evangelize this world for Kingdom of God purposes. Get this in your spirit—it is your Christian duty and critical to the soul of this nation to enforce the principles of God through your apostolate. The first step toward reformation is embracing a sense of duty.

> *And having a readiness to revenge all disobedience, when your obedience is fulfilled* (2 Corinthians 10:6 KJV).

*Readiness* is the Greek word *hetoimos,* and it means "to be fit, prepared, and ready" (Strong, G2092). *To revenge* is the Greek word *ekdikeo,* meaning "to vindicate, retaliate, enforce, punish, avenge" (Strong, G1556).

The apostle Paul says an apostolate must be ready to retaliate with decrees of faith to plant the heavens until faith is sowed into the earth. His message implores believers to be fit and ready to enforce what God says—to be active warriors and to fight for what is divine. Clearly the apostolic call is for aggressive Christianity and not passive appeasement.

The original language of Second Corinthians 10:3-6 is so powerful. Hear it as originally intended: "Submit and comply to the will of God, manifesting your Christian faith by being fit and ready to enforce and avenge words contrary to God's words. Be actively engaged warriors, prepared to retaliate when necessary and always ready to extend completely and fully through your own obedience the strategies of your apostolates that pull down enemy strongholds. Be engaged and ready at all times to execute your Christian duties with aggressive faith."

What a statement. Certainly the New Testament church in Colossae, Corinth, Ephesus, and in Philippi understood that they were at war. We cannot allow the world to define us. We must have God and His Word define us.

# HOLY SPIRIT,

*What a privilege it is to steward Heaven's strategies in my life, my family and my nation! As Your church, help us take new responsibility to see Your principles established and the strongholds of the enemy pulled down. Lead us to be actively engaged warriors, seeing Your Kingdom made manifest and Your name glorified.*

# THE SPECIAL FORCES
# OF THE KINGDOM

> **I DECREE** I am strong in the Lord
> and in the power of His might.

From the world's view, Christians are supposed to be peaceful and loving and turn the other cheek. Personally, I will turn the other cheek when wronged, but I will not turn my cheek to cultural sin and disobedience to God's Word. We are never told to, nor will I, submit to ungodliness. We want peace, but not at the exclusion of contending for God's principles.

In Ephesians 5:11-12, Paul issues very aggressive warfare commands. These Scriptures are written to frontline soldiers equipped by the five-fold ministry. They are not written to someone who pacifies or appeases their opposition. He then moves to Ephesians 6 and gives the ekklesia another very aggressive command. It is a command that we must engage in our times: *"Finally, my brethren, be strong in the Lord, and in the power of his might"* (Ephesians 6:10 KJV).

*Finally* is the descriptive word *loipon* in the Greek language, and though it is the first word of the statement, it does not mean "lastly." We need to focus on what Paul is trying to convey to us here. *Loipon* means "something remaining, remaining ones, or a remnant" (Strong, G3063). You almost have to shout this text to read it correctly. "Remnant warriors; those who do not run; those who do not quit; those who do not scatter, those who stand; those who remain, those who make a stand." The apostle Paul begins with a declaration to remnant warriors—to the Triumphant Reserve. He exhorts, "Be strong, remnant ones; be strong, remnant warriors."

Our military today has soldiers in the regular army, but it also has Special Forces units. We have Army Rangers and Navy Seals. They are "bad to the bone" dudes. Don't mess with them. *Loipon* is the word for the special forces units of the Kingdom of God. They are "bad to the bone" spiritual warfare soldiers. Don't mess with them because they are engaging themselves through a Kingdom ekklesia.

Paul says, "Remnant warriors, *loipon*, special forces units in the Kingdom of God, be strong in the Lord and in the power of His might." *Lord* is the Greek word *kyrios,* meaning "master, superintendent, controller, and supreme in authority" (Strong, G2962). So be strong in the supreme authority of the Lord. Be strong in the Master's delegated authority. Remnant warriors, superintend and control with your authority.

*Power* is the Greek word *kratos,* meaning "to manifest evident force, activated forces, and dominion" (Strong, G2904). This is Paul's reference to the dominion mandate in Genesis 1:26-28 when God commands man to have dominion over every living thing and subdue the earth. Paul is calling for the remnant to dominate with Christ's supreme authority. It's part of your Christian duty.

*Might* is the Greek word *ischus,* and it means "ability, capacity, prevail" (Strong, G2479). Paul says be strong in the Lord's abilities that are freely delegated to you. Move in His capacities, prevailing, superintending, and dominating principalities, powers, mights, and dominions. Rise up within your apostolates and dominate demons. Paul would have been hard-pressed to use stronger language.

## LORD GOD,

*I pray for Your ways and principles to be established on earth, bringing reformation into every part of society. May Your church rise now in new strength and focus to establish righteousness by the authority You have given us. We will not submit to ungodliness, but instead stand firm in the truth of Your powerful Word.*

# BATTLING AT THE GATES

> **WE DECREE** the church is the strongest force on earth. We declare that we will fight until we win and see reformation in Jesus' name.

In Bible days, the city gate was like our nation's capital, Washington, D.C., or a state capital such as Columbus for Ohio. Business was transacted at the gate. Legislation was enacted at the gate. The ekklesia is to take the battle to the gate of our country.

David, king of Israel, was one of God's greatest warriors, and he governed and made laws. Still, he was a man after God's own heart, and he had God's approval. Moses was a lawgiver establishing ethical codes of conduct, laws, and penalties for societal violations. The Book of Judges is about the judges who governed and yet were great men and women of God. Solomon, Deborah, Hezekiah, Gideon, Joseph, Joshua, Saul, Josiah, and Daniel influenced government as well as moral and civic laws or codes of conduct. Esther and Mordecai rewrote laws and prophesied into their government to influence moral and civic laws and codes of conduct. Elijah, Elisha, Samuel, Jeremiah, Isaiah, Nathan, Nehemiah, Hosea, Amos, Obadiah, Ezekiel, Micah, and John the Baptist also did. Paul spoke to leaders and governors of Rome. Stephen, James, and Peter did as well. Where in the world did we get the notion that we are to stay out of the government? It is demon doctrine meant to muzzle the church and kill America as well as other nations of the world. The church is expected to be present at the regional and national gates addressing leaders, governors, and presidents in a manner that brings glory to God.

Clearly our call is to attack the powers of hell through prayer and faith decrees. Followers of Christ are here to war against hell's leadership and to stop its business in the earth today. Our Lord says He will build His church and the gates of hell will not prevail against it (see Matt. 16:18).

We have a responsibility to respond aggressively against some things. We're not supposed to be in favor of everything. Consider Ephesians 6:10-12. Paul said the word *against* four times when associated with principalities, powers, the rulers of the darkness of this world, and spiritual wickedness in high places. Paul is saying, "Remnant warriors, if you encounter principalities, step forward; don't back up, don't march in place. Step forward. If you see powers, step forward. And if you see spiritual wickedness in high places (which refers to the leadership of hell itself, lucifer), don't back down. You have dominating authority over him; step forward. Rule and reign with the King. In Him is the strength for warfare."

Understand that the strength that God gives us is not for some kind of spiritual style show, but it is strength to do battle for Him at the gates. The church is the strongest force on earth. That strength must be used as God intended. We cannot waste it.

**JESUS,**

*I bless Your church today. I bless Your church to battle for You at the gates of our communities, nations and families. With fresh vision, I declare that the church is the strongest force on earth and in Your name, we will release Your realities into every realm of society. We will rule and reign with You, King Jesus!*

# THE BORN-AGAIN NATURE

> **I DECREE** God's seed, sown in me, is producing His character and tendencies in my life.

God's seed sown into your heart produces God because it produces after its kind. It's a law of perpetuity. A God-seed produces His genetic codes in your spirit. You really are a son or daughter of God. Through the parenting seed, character traits, mannerisms, tendencies, and likes or dislikes are passed on to the offspring. Preferences, actions, and hereditary dispositions are inherited through the parents' seed. This is true in our own family, as it is in yours. My daughter, Rachel, and I both can't talk without using our hands. We also have very similar temperaments. Our son, Joshua, is very much like his mother. They have similar personalities and leadership skills. It's interesting and fun to notice these things.

If God's seed is in us, then certain tendencies of His will be passed on. It's why believers whose minds are renewed by God's Word can believe that miracles are still possible on the earth. Why? Because we're God's seed; we are His children, and He is the miracle-worker. It is sown into our new nature to have that leaning.

The world does not believe that all things are possible. But Christians whose minds are renewed by God's Word can easily believe such a thing. It's a hereditary trait inside of us. We tend to express power. Why? It's in our nature. It was seeded into us at our new birth. We tend to think with authority. We are predisposed that way because God's parenting seed is in us, and He is the highest authority. He has passed that on to us. We tend to believe for dominion, to see ourselves ruling, reigning, and conquering. These are hereditary leanings in the redeemed ones because we're God's seed. His disposition as the ruler of all is planted into us, into our nature, and it's very real. This is why First John 4:4 (AMP) says, *"You are of God and you belong to Him and have [already] overcome them [the agents of the antichrist]; because He who is in you is greater than he (satan) who is in the world [of sinful mankind]."*

God is in us. He has planted His seed into us through His Word. His disposition to always overcome evil is planted into our very nature as a part of our spiritual DNA. He has seeded into the nature of His children to never give up but rather to subdue, conquer, and reign in Jesus' name.

There have been many situations in my life over the years when it would have been so much easier to just give up and quit. These times were so chaotic that others suggested that I give up and move on. But quitting is not in my born-again nature. It's not in the hereditary leanings my Father put into me. There is always the possibility to conquer and overcome with Him if I don't give up. Because of the hereditary nature deep inside of me, I didn't give up, and many times I won what was impossible in the natural realm. God put no losing seed in you!

## HOLY SPIRIT,

*Thank You that I am born again through Your powerful seed! Thank You that Your DNA lives inside of me and that my born-again nature gets to determine the situations in my life. Teach me to experience the outworking of Your parenting seed inside of me as Your character is reproduced in my life.*

# PLANT THE HEAVENS

> **WE DECREE** the rightful rule of King Jesus over the earth, the region and over the kingdom of darkness.

Years ago, before I ever understood that words are seeds, I remember I was asked to go to a very small church in southern Ohio. I don't remember what the event was, but I remember praying, "OK, Lord. What should I share with these people?" As I prayed about, it I received revelation concerning the church ruling and reigning with Christ Jesus in this life (see Rom. 5:17).

God said, *"I need you to plant this word into the region."* I began to think, "Can I do that? Lord, can I plant a message in the heavens and the earth realm of a region? Do You really want me to plant a message, to plant doctrine from Your Word into the atmosphere of a region?"

This method of planting the heavens was also taught by Jesus. Remember that He first planted the heavens and the earth in Genesis 1. He is the Word. He planted the entire universe with word seed decrees, saying "be" and it was.

When Jesus walked the earth, we see that His words just caused things to happen. Wherever He went, He opened His mouth and He sounded forth decrees that brought miraculous results. In John 6:63 (NKJV) He tells us, saying this, *"The words that I speak to you are spirit, and they are life."* Understand the magnitude of that statement. When Christ spoke, when He opened His mouth and decreed, Holy Spirit moved into the atmosphere. His mouth opened the atmosphere for Holy Spirit to begin to move. Remember, Holy Spirit hovers until He hears the Word of God. When He hears the Word of God declared, He moves, just like He did upon the chaos and darkness in the beginning.

Christ's mouth opened ways for the Kingdom to come. His mouth proclaimed an invitation, "Holy Spirit come. Move here."

What Jesus said produced after its kind. The superior reality of the Kingdom of God, a spiritual Kingdom that visibly affects the entire earth, began to move and transform the earth realm. The Word became a reality and produced what He decreed. The seed in the words produced it. Jesus was modeling ministry for you and me, His joint heirs.

When the sons and daughters of God open their mouths and decree God's Word, it can change the atmosphere of a region. Our decrees act as a catalyst that sets in motion a chain of events to bring God's Word to pass. They open the heavens so blessings can rain down, miracles can be produced, and we can receive revelation and enlightenment. Our decrees attract angel armies to ascend and descend and assist the heirs of salvation in that region (see Heb. 1:14).

As God's heirs, as His children on the earth, we are commissioned to plant the heavens with His words, to seed them with declarations of truth. We must declare, on the basis of God's Word, the rightful rule of King Jesus over the earth, the region, and over the kingdom of darkness. We are commissioned to do it.

**JESUS,**

*You spoke and saw the superior reality of the Kingdom of God made manifest. I ask for You to teach me how to do the same. You modeled a ministry that was possible for me to walk in. Teach me how to decree Your word and see the atmosphere shift in my region.*

# OUR BORN-AGAIN DNA

**WE DECREE** that as sons and daughters of God, we will reign in His name, speaking words of life and revival.

Have you ever wondered why you feel so different from the rest of the world? Do you ever think that those around you who are not born again seem like foreigners? It's like they speak a foreign language. Where did they come up with those crazy ideas? But you know they believe the things they say. Do you ever wonder why you think so differently? It's because you have inherited genetic leanings that cause you to think differently. You're God's seed, His child. It is in you to be different. In fact, if you live contrary to God's seed, your conscience is going to bother you because the Holy Spirit in you is going to say, "No, stop it. Don't do that. That's not who you are." You are His child.

Your Father's likes and dislikes have been passed on to you. God's character traits are at work in you, desiring to grow and mature. *You're an heir of God and a joint heir with Christ Jesus* (see Rom. 8:17). Renew your mind to it. Transform your thinking by meditating on who God's Word says you really are. Practice Paul's admonition in Romans 12:2 (AMP):

> *And do not be conformed to this world [any longer with its superficial values and customs], but be transformed and progressively changed [as you mature spiritually] by the renewing of your mind [focusing on godly values and ethical attitudes], so that you may prove [for yourselves] what the will of God is, that which is good and acceptable and perfect [in His plan and purpose for you].*

We need to reprogram our minds to think like children of God. To think like one born into a dynasty family of governing authority—the

God dynasty. We must think like one living the mandate of God to exercise dominion upon the earth in His name, activating real Christian living.

Amazingly, God wants to reproduce Himself in you. He wants His image, likeness, and life to grow in you. He wants you to rule and reign with Him. You were born of God to have dominion, not to be dominated by hell, society, culture, or government. Your DNA reads *Overcomer*. Your DNA says *Dominator*. Your DNA declares *Ruler with my Father*. He wants you to be an activated heir, restored in purpose and identity as His offspring to create with words that agree with His words. Like your Father, you as a child of God create with words that are seeds.

As His seed on the earth, He wants you to create with "word seed" decrees—create atmospheres for miracles, parameters for society to live in, and an environment that produces life and destroys death. Father God wants His seed in you to release His creative abilities upon the earth.

If you have confessed Jesus as Lord, He has germinated His nature as a seed inside of you. You really are a child of God. A part of your restored purpose is to seed the world with His words. Never speak negative words or unbelief. They are contrary to the seed of God that is in you. Reign in His name, speaking words of life and revival. We are here as His sons and His daughters to voice His Word everywhere. The greatest days in church history are not in our past; they are in our present and in our future. Say what God says.

## LORD JESUS,

*Thank You for calling Your born-again ones Your sons and daughters! Fill our mouths with words of life and revival that we may see the atmosphere shift around us. Prompt us, Holy Spirit, to seed the world with Your powerful word seeds that we may reap an abundant harvest for You!*

# THE AWAKENED EKKLESIA

> **WE DECREE** an anointing of
> boldness is rising in the body of Christ.

Recently, I was pondering and seeking the Lord for strategies for our times in this new era. A constant prayer of mine is, "What is the present word of the Lord?" I was contemplating Holy Spirit's move in this new era with His angel armies and the remnant now forming an active ekklesia, a reigning church moving in power and glory under greater authority than we have ever seen.

I began to pray about this in the spirit, using my heavenly prayer language. As I prayed, I began pondering the very first ekklesia Jesus ever built in Acts 2, and I began to see many of the precedents initiated in the first ekklesia now beginning to build in our times.

Then, and this is a bit unusual for me, I began to interpret what I was praying in the spirit. This was in a private time of prayer, not a corporate time. The ending part of what I interpreted was the apostles' prayer in Christ's first Kingdom ekklesia in Acts 4:29. It rose up out of my spirit: "Grant that great boldness would be upon us to preach Your Word and give us signs, wonders, and miracles in the name of Jesus." I just kept repeating that. The first ekklesia in Christ's Kingdom prayed for boldness to confront adversarial culture, government, and religion, and we certainly need a similar anointing today.

Perhaps you've noticed there's a lot of animosity currently directed at the true church. Our values are demeaned and ridiculed by much of society. The church has been pronounced as irrelevant and the demise of the church is often stated.

I was pondering all of this and began to pray the prayer of the first apostles in the first ekklesia. God, give us boldness to speak Your Word like never before. Boldness to declare what Your Word says without any compromise. I especially like how *The Message* records their prayer:

> *And now they're at it again! Take care of their threats and give your servants fearless confidence in preaching your Message, as you stretch out your hand to us in healings and miracles and wonders done in the name of your holy servant Jesus." While they were praying, the place where they were meeting trembled and shook. They were all filled with the Holy Spirit and continued to speak God's Word with fearless confidence* (Acts 4:29-31 MSG).

After praying, "Lord, give us bold, fearless confidence to declare Your Word. Give us miracles, signs, and wonders," I then stated a very simple prayer, "Holy Spirit, what are You saying to the church? What are You doing right now?"

Holy Spirit answered immediately and there was a boldness in His voice that I instantly recognized. There was actually a conviction and a determination in His voice that I could feel.

Holy Spirit said, "We're preparing to show the world the strength of the Lord of Hosts. He is tired of His sons and daughters being bullied. The strong arm of the Lord will now be seen overpowering and defeating the forever loser through the awakened ekklesia."

### GOD,

*I pray for Your church today. I pray for a fearless confidence to arise in her. Like the early church, please grant us a fresh boldness to speak Your word without compromise. May our actions reveal the strength of the Lord of Hosts!*

# FROM GLORY TO GLORY

> **WE DECREE** everything in the Kingdom of God
> is accelerating. We decree all prophetic words are
> coming to their moment of activation in Jesus' name.

It is amazing how Holy Spirit can instantly download revelation that is extensive. Sometimes, it's like trying to get a drink from a fire hose.

Holy Spirit spoke with a bold voice inside of me, and I wrote as quickly as I could, *"My ekklesia is now entering the times when prophetic words are intersecting their moment in accelerated ways. Prophetic words are intersecting their fullness of time, their due season. They have come to their activation moment and their assignment will now accelerate forward."*

This was similar to a word given to me June 20, 2017. I was awakened about three o'clock in the morning with Holy Spirit saying:

> My ekklesia is now entering a fullness of time. A fresh new Pentecost will now be poured out. The precedent set in its foundations will now be seen in the remnant, and everything in My Kingdom will now accelerate. Begin to decree that the apostolic precedents in My first ekklesia will now accelerate.

Be encouraged; everything is accelerating. I know many do not see it because troubling times tend to fog it up, but in Christ's Kingdom it is building and building quickly. The people in Acts 2 did not see it initially, either. Remember, the first apostles themselves wanted to quit before receiving the power and fire of God.

Some considered going back to their old occupations, but a world-shaking, world-shaping event happened as prophesied, and the same thing is happening in our times. The true church isn't fading away into the sunset. No, the precedent is clear. We're going from glory to glory as Paul said in Second Corinthians 3:18. This must somehow mean bigger and bigger, or better and better, or stronger and stronger. It cannot mean weaker and weaker until we crawl off of this planet like whipped puppies. I'm not crawling anywhere. Like Shadrach, Meshach, and Abednego, I will not bow.

Our King and our brilliant strategist, Holy Spirit, have the greatest days in church history planned. Holy Spirit said prophetic words are connecting to their moment, thousands of them.

Then Holy Spirit continued with a prophetic declaration that surged inside of me, saying:

> Prophetic words have now intersected their moment, and the ekklesia (New Testament church) must activate them with decrees of faith. As they do, angels of Christ's Kingdom government that I have now moved to the battlefronts will assist the ekklesia's decrees to produce rapidly. Production in the Kingdom of God will now accelerate. I will empower their decrees and they will come to pass. You have entered the new day. A new era is before you...."

## LORD,

*I believe Your prophetic declaration. I believe that the greatest days in church history are upon us and that Your prophetic words and promises are connecting to their moment. As these promises are now accelerating, help me anchor and action my faith, aligning with what You have said.*

# MESSIAH THE BREAKER

> **WE DECREE** Messiah the Breaker is going before us and we will break through.

*The Breaker [the Messiah] will go up before them. They will break through, pass in through the gate and go out through it, and their King will pass on before them, the Lord at their head* (Micah 2:13 AMPC).

Please notice King Jesus is identified as King Breaker who goes before us to ensure our breakthrough. He leads us through *gates,* which is the Hebrew word *shaar,* which means "doors" (Strong's H8179). Doors to new areas, opportunities, places, or lands. It represents a way through.

Jesus is the way opener. He goes before His people to break up obstacles, opening the way to new promised territories, inheritance, and destiny (both individual and corporate). The one who plans your destiny goes before you, breaking you free from any hinderance to that destiny.

The word *breaker* is the Hebrew word *parats* and it means "to break out, to burst out, to grow out, to grow through something" (Strong's H6555). It's like a seed that grows up out of the dirt and, as it does, it will break out and produce what it is. It's similar to a child who grows out of his/her clothes. This kind of breakthrough comes as a result of growth. You grow up and out.

Also, *parats* means to increase in spiritual strength until you're strong enough to break something. *Parats* means "the one who breaks up, goes before to give you strength to breakthrough." Breakthrough is the Hebrew word *abar* and it means "passover or crossover" (Strong's H5674). According to Hebrew scholar Spiros Zodhiates, *parats* can also means "to impregnate with concepts, ideas, or purposes." *Parats* means "the seed is planted and it goes through the growth process."

Although there are many types of breakthrough, let me reference three of them for you:

- Suddenly. Some breakthrough is simply the busting up of situations or hinderances, etc. God comes, He breaks it up, and you're free. It's a suddenly.

- Grow your way out of. Other breakthroughs you must grow your way out of, with His assistance. To achieve supernatural breakthrough, you may have to acquire spiritual strength and growth to break out.

- Impregnate your soul. Some breakthrough comes from God impregnating your soul with something that you must nourish in the womb of your soul, until it's time for it to break out and live outside in the world.

I've seen all three types of breakthrough in my life over the years. If you've been a Christian for any length of time, you've probably experienced all three of these. There've been times when the Lord just simply broke things up and I was free. There have been plenty of other breakthroughs where the Holy Spirit has helped me grow my way through. I had to strengthen myself in the spirit, growing my faith, getting rid of any areas of unbelief or any issues that I needed to, and then He led me to the doors of breakthrough.

Some breakthroughs have resulted in God impregnating my soul with possibilities, dreams, ideas, concepts, callings, and prophecies. These three types of breakthroughs occur in seasons of outpourings overseen by Holy Spirit, Jesus the Breaker, and assisted by breakthrough angels.

## JESUS,

*You are the Breaker! Thank You for going before me to prepare the way. Thank You that Your breakthrough angels are assisting You to open doors of opportunity and unlock new promised territories. In Your kindness, You prepare my destiny and then remove any obstacle that prevents me from getting there. I am so grateful.*

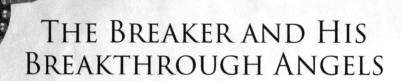

# THE BREAKER AND HIS BREAKTHROUGH ANGELS

> **WE DECREE** that when the King
> comes in, everything changes.

The apostle Paul taught that the Greeks always believed that the spirit realm was more real than the natural because the spirit realm is eternal, while the natural is only temporary. It's like getting a drop of water out of a pond, which you drop onto a glass slide and view through a microscope. Suddenly, you see there's a world going on in that drop of water that you didn't see with your natural eyes. It was always there, but you had to have the right equipment to see it. The same is true of the spirit realm. It is very real, but only Holy Spirit can anoint you to see into it. He does this through a gift described in First Corinthians 12 as the discerning of spirits.

I began to see a vision in the spirit realm recently that I had seen many times over the last couple of years—of breakthrough angels that accompany Messiah the Breaker. There are millions of these break-through angels in this division. Micah 2:13 says Messiah the Breaker will go before us and we will break through. When Jesus went to the cross, He said He had 72,000 (six legions) of these angels with Him, and if He wanted to break out of this He could, but He submitted to the plan of God. Clearly, breakthrough angels accompany Him.

Each angel carried what looked like a long wooden mallet, similar to a sledgehammer. They would strike the ground, hitting it so hard I could feel the thud of it. You could feel the vibrations as the angels struck the ground, making their decrees of *"Break up! Break out! Break through!"* They repeated this over and over.

One particular Sunday morning at The Oasis, I saw breakthrough angels lined up around the sanctuary, striking the ground with huge wooden mallets. Our worship leader, who is my daughter, Rachel, was singing a song of the Lord at the time: "One, two, three, four, as they strike the ground, He's breaking open doors." I saw an enormous angel to my right holding out a huge mallet. When I turned back, I saw many other angels around the sanctuary striking the ground with their mallets declaring, "Break up, break out, break through."

At this point, Rachel transitioned to the next song and began singing, "When He walks into the room." At that point, the huge angel to my right put his mallet down by his side and the other angels, seeing him do this, put their mallets down by their sides and bowed their heads in reverence to the Breaker. Of course, these actions signified their understanding that the important One is the Breaker Himself. They are just serving Him to bring us breakthrough. At this point, I felt the atmosphere of the room shift completely, and as the tangible presence of the King Himself came into the room I began to weep. I was recognizing how much these angels were reverencing the Lord Jesus, our Breaker. There is absolutely nothing like the presence of the Breaker Himself, not even the presence of angels. When the King comes in, everything changes.

## LORD JESUS,

*Thank You that Your breakthrough angels are constantly working to bring Your word to come to pass. Thank You for their help and assistance in my life. More than anything, thank You that they remind me of You, the Breaker. When You come, everything changes.*

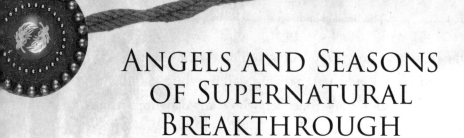

# Angels and Seasons of Supernatural Breakthrough

> **WE DECREE** break up, break out, break through, passover, and possess.

I woke up on Passover morning (April 8, 2020) and was blind in my right eye. I couldn't see anything, not even my hand in front of my face. My wife, Carol, said I needed to see a doctor and find out what was going on.

After running various tests for several hours, they determined I had a virus in my eye and gave me four prescriptions. The next morning, as I was getting ready for some podcast interviews in my office, I was praying and talking to the Lord when a thought crossed my mind: "I wonder if this is prophetic?" This had been so unusual. I knew God hadn't done this to me, but I was wondering if He wanted to speak to me through this.

I said, "Holy Spirit, do You have something to say to me concerning the vision of the apostolic or prophetic being attacked?" As soon as I prayed that, I was instantly in the spirit. I don't even know how to describe it, but if you have ever had it happen you know it's as if you just stepped into a different realm. I could see things in the spirit. I saw in the spirit realm a host of breaker angels. The angels were striking the ground and decreeing, "Break up. Break out. Break through. Passover. Possess."

I had never heard Holy Spirit have the angels use these two words in this way—*passover* and *possess*. I began to understand a major shift is taking place in the spirit realm. The Breaker Himself and His Holy

Spirit have plans, and His angels are being activated and are going forth into this world to break up, break out, break through. They are enabling us to passover and possess our inheritance. They are being released by the millions upon this planet to assist us in awesome breakthrough.

It is our time to break out and passover into an inheritance in new ways at new levels. We've come into a fullness of time—meaning "prophetic words, dreams, and visions are now connecting to their moment. Our prayers are hitting the mark; they have been heard and Heaven is answering. The ekklesia is being seated with an anointing to prevail. They are being seated with Christ's authority, declared from their lips at levels the world has never seen before. There is boldness and their decrees of faith are being heard, activating and permitting some things on earth and deactivating or forbidding others. We're entering seasons of supernatural breakthrough. They will happen in your life and in churches everywhere.

At the end of hearing the angels of breakthrough decree, "Break up. Break out. Break through. Passover. Possess," I then heard a starting pistol being fired like you would hear at the beginning of a race. No one shouts *run*; the pistol itself prophesies *run*. It is time to run with King Jesus. It's time to run into breakthrough, to run to the battle and see the success we have been promised. It's time to run with Messiah our Breaker.

## HOLY SPIRIT,

*Thank You that Your breakthrough angels are now moving on our behalf to allow us to passover and possess our inheritance. I believe our prayers are now hitting the mark and Heaven is responding to the intercession of the saints. I posture my heart to see You afresh and experience this season of supernatural breakthrough in Jesus' name.*

# ANOINTED TO PREVAIL

**WE DECREE** that we are being anointed to prevail and we are entering the seasons of supernatural breakthrough.

Micah 2:13 says, "Then I, God, will burst all confinements." It is the season for confinement to break as Messiah the Breaker goes before us as His Kingdom advances. The confinements and constraints upon the true church are now going to be supernaturally broken. Millions of promises will now spring up and break free—no more confinement and no more delay. The breaker angels accompanying Him have heard the King's decree to break confinement. When we stop listening with our natural ears to what the world is saying and start listening with our spiritual ears, we will hear the chains of disease, poverty, fear, bondage, and depression break.

> *The Breaker [the Messiah] will go up before them. They will break through, pass in through the gate and go out through it, and their King will pass on before them, the Lord at their head* (Micah 2:13 AMPC).

*Alah* is the Hebrew word for "go up" and is used over 900 times in the Old Testament (Strong's H5927). It means "to mount up, to rise up, to lead up." *Alah* also means "to go from a lower elevation to a higher one." It pictures, in the Hebrew language, sheep being led by their shepherd to a higher feeding area. *Anago* also means "to mount up, rise up, or to go to a higher elevation" (Strong's G321). In Matthew 4:1, we read that Jesus was *led up* by the Holy Spirit to a mountain, where He fasted and prayed for 40 days, overcoming the devil's attack. Both Micah 2:13 and Matthew 4:1 are describing Jesus the Messiah. In the Old and the New Testaments, Messiah the Breaker is described as one who takes sheep to a higher level.

*Anago* and *alah* give clear prophetic meaning to us today. The identity of Messiah the Breaker prophesies to us that He will give breakthrough after breakthrough so that we can go to higher and higher levels in life, relationships, purpose, and ministry. There is a remnant with a willingness to follow the Breaker and come on up in order to advance Christ's Kingdom to a new level on the earth.

Our King Jesus is rising now as Jehovah *Parats,* the Breaker, with Heaven's division of breakthrough angels. We're entering the seasons of supernatural breakthrough. They will happen in your life and in churches everywhere. The attacks against the prophetic and apostolic vision will backfire. God is restoring clear vision, leading to the greatest harvest we have ever seen, confirmed by signs, wonders, and miracles.

The call of the King and the Holy Spirit is to press upward to higher levels of ministry, purpose, and a greater calling. The Messiah is leading us into a supernatural breakthrough season. Step forward by faith and believe that confinement is going to break off of your life. Press in and come on up to higher ground, into greater glory, worship, and destiny. Thankfully, we have millions of angels in the breakthrough division to assist us in going to higher ground. Assisting us to break up, break out, break through, passover, possess.

### JESUS,

*You are leading us into a season of supernatural breakthrough. Give us the grace to press in and come to higher ground with You. Thank You for your angels that are assisting us now to go to new levels of glory. Thank You for their help as we break up, break out, break through, passover and possess!*

# THE NEW PENTECOST

> **WE DECREE** every yoke of bondage is broken.
> God is changing our times and our seasons.

When I received the vision of the breakthrough angels, I recalled what Prophet Chuck Pierce had prophesied in 2019 concerning a literal Passover that would occur in 2020. This happened; the entire world passed over a coronavirus pandemic, a literal plague.

Just as Moses had told the people to stay in their homes during the first Passover, Benjamin Netanyahu, the Prime Minister of Israel, announced in April 2020 a nationwide lockdown during the end of the Passover holiday. And, just as Moses and the Israelites passed out of Egyptian bondage with the armies of the Lord accompanying them (see Exod. 12:41), we, too, are going to see the releasing of angel armies on assignment to break us through into new land.

As all of this was occurring, I heard Holy Spirit say to me:

> Just as Passover will be a literal Passover, Pentecost will be a literal Pentecost.

Pentecost activates a yoke-destroying anointing so we can break out and break free. It doesn't just break the yoke, it destroys it according to Isaiah 10:27 (NKJV): *"It shall come to pass in that day that his burden will be taken away from your shoulder, and his yoke from your neck, and the yoke will be destroyed because of the anointing oil."* Something that is merely broken can be fixed, but God says, "My anointing *destroys* yokes."

A yoke is a wooden bar that fits over the neck of oxen, or other beasts of burden, and joins them with a leather strap, so they can work together. With the yoke in place, the oxen are used to plow through fields or to pull heavy wagons.

God says, "I'm going to pour out my anointing and destroy the yokes that have bound you. You're entering into a time when you won't have to plow everywhere you go or drag heavy burdens around with you. I'm activating a new Pentecost, and I'm going to release a deluge of anointing that obliterates yokes of bondage so My people can move into new territories of blessings, hope, and harvest."

Pentecost is all about God changing times and seasons. This is a part of what the new Pentecost is about—an ability and an anointing enabling us to produce beyond the natural realm. We're not limited to natural abilities. Holy Spirit comes, activating divine ability, empowering us to do what we cannot do in and of ourselves. This particular season of Pentecost is also about God birthing some things on the earth that Holy Spirit has planned and that King Breaker and His breakthrough angels will lead us into.

God's Word teaches us that the first New Testament Pentecost in Acts 2 was about birthing—the first ekklesia, the first Kingdom of God and government of Christ's heirs, a great move of God, an abundant harvest, the fivefold ministry, and activation of the saints to do the work of the ministry. The Pentecost we are now cycling into is the same—we are entering into a mega-birthing season. There are things that He has impregnated into His Kingdom that have now come to calving season; they are due.

GOD,

*You alone change times and seasons. I believe that You are birthing something new in the earth, releasing a new Pentecost and moving in ways the world has never seen before. Thank You that as You move, You are destroying yokes of bondage and clearing the way for Your church to move forward into new realms of blessing and harvest.*

# From Pregnant Pause to Worldwide Revival

> **WE DECREE** the birth of a new
> Kingdom of God movement on the earth.

In the last few weeks of a pregnancy, you pause a bit, slowing down and not moving around as much. It's not because anything is wrong, but because it's right, and the time to deliver is close. You're waiting, but with expectancy. A pregnant pause is a pause preceding birth to strengthen and prepare what is about to be birthed. You could have a baby at six or seven months, but it would be fragile and would require a lot of care. Typically, if you can nourish the baby and rest the last few weeks of the pregnancy, the child will be born ready to thrive.

The dictionary definition of a pregnant pause can also refer to building anticipation for a declaration, a revealing of something, a mission or a goal that you wish to emphasize, or an answer to something. A pregnant pause signifies the importance of what is to be revealed, or the importance of a goal about to be stated or activated.

Pentecost is about birthing a movement and generating supernatural power that man doesn't have in and of himself. Prophetically, we have moved from a pregnant pause to a mega Pentecost. We will now see the birth of a new Kingdom of God movement on this planet like has never been seen before. All of the past moves are activating anew in a fresh anointing of the Holy Spirit to function at higher levels, along with all the new concepts, places, territories, and prophetic destinies that Holy Spirit has planned. This will all be done in a spiritual atmosphere of far greater glory.

There will never be a time when God's manifestation will be as clear as it will be now. The presence of God will be felt and seen. This will birth a functioning ekklesia, one that has been trained and nurtured in the soul of a remnant. This ekklesia is due to be birthed on this planet and is a game changer. We will stare hell in the face and not back down. We will see signs, wonders, and miracles that will activate the power of God on this earth at levels that have been ordained through the prophets.

We're moving from a pregnant pause to a worldwide revival that is being birthed to answer a global pandemic of sin, rebellion, and iniquity. Holy Spirit impregnated Christ's Kingdom with all that is needed for Messiah the Breaker to lead us through doors to His greatest move in all of history. He is supplying breakthrough angels to assist us in accomplishing His plans, and they will be released in this new-era Pentecost.

A remnant has been nurturing and strengthening those promises in the wombs of their souls, not letting it go. We've held on to them, fed them, and decreed them. They will grow to fullness, ripen, and be birthed.

We're going to see a breakthrough and a birthing of hopes, dreams, concepts, goals, promises, and visions. We've come to the time and Pentecost is coming to give us strength to deliver it. The strategies hell has attempted will now backfire.

## LORD JESUS,

*I declare that my heart is ready for what You are birthing on the earth! Your promises have been nurtured and now is the time for them to come forth. Align our hearts to what You are doing and what You are bringing to fruition. May the world see and experience a fresh move of Your Spirit that brings worldwide breakthrough and harvest.*

# TRAINING TO REIGNING

**WE DECREE** the greatest surge of the Kingdom of
God overcoming the kingdom of darkness. We decree
we are now leaving training time for reigning time.

Holy Spirit is coming to pour out power from Heaven. He's coming
to pour out an anointing to prevail. Just as the precedent reveals in the
previous Pentecosts, He is coming with the hosts of Heaven, bringing
angel armies with Him in far greater measure.

The division of breakthrough angels will accompany Him to assist
us in breaking out into the greatest move of God on the planet. Also,
angels of awakening, revival, healings and miracles, deliverance, communication, enlightening, and war are coming with Him.

He promised this literal Pentecost, which is far more than just a
single day, would begin an era of outpouring after outpouring, replenishing outpourings. He promised that He was bringing division after
division of angel armies to the battle lines to assist our breakthroughs
and victories.

Today's outpouring will not be localized to a particular nation or
church. This one will be the first Kingdom-wide outpouring, which has
never before happened. The outpouring of the Book of Acts birthed the
church and Christ's Kingdom, but that Kingdom was small and func-
tioned locally, at least in its beginning. But now, it's global. Now, ekklesias are decreeing God's Word into regions everywhere. Now, the heirs
of God and joint heirs with Christ understand their authority.

By necessity, by the sheer number of saints and churches, this outpouring must be far greater, and it will be. The plan of God is to soak

a Kingdom of ekklesias with power from on high. His plan is to assist them with millions of angels, in multiple divisions, operating under Holy Spirit guidance. His plan is to overwhelm the forces of hell with a worldwide outpouring. Hell has never before faced anything like it.

This will activate a worldwide move of God that hell can't stop. Everywhere it attempts to advance, it will face an ekklesia and its angel armies, empowered and led by Holy Spirit. This era of Pentecost outpourings will also activate Holy Ghost and fire, setting ablaze a worldwide revival—a billion-soul harvest, at the least—and angels are coming to help us reap it.

> *He answered and said to them: "He who sows the good seed is the Son of Man. The field is the world, the good seeds are the sons of the kingdom, but the tares are the sons of the wicked one. The enemy who sowed them is the devil, the harvest is the end of the age, and the reapers are the angels"* (Matthew 13:37-39 NKJV).

We are now leaving training time for reigning time.

## HOLY SPIRIT,

*I am ready for a fresh outpouring of Your presence. Thank You that what You are releasing now is not localized, but it is for global impact. Thank You that Your angels are assisting Your ekklesia to rule and reign with You. You have promised us a new Pentecost and as the early church did, we believe you and wait in expectation for Your Spirit to come.*

# ANGEL ASSISTANCE AND THE MEGA-PENTECOST

**WE DECREE** a new Pentecost is anointing us for supernatural acceleration. We decree power from Heaven is anointing us to see signs, wonders, miracles, and great harvest.

We are living in one of the most opportune and strategic times in Christian history. We are moving by divine plan into a mega-Pentecost outpouring of the Holy Spirit. This will activate and release supernatural anointing for God's people to prevail. It will also release many of the promises for which the true church has been believing. This will be true both corporately and individually. This mega-Pentecost will activate the release of millions of angels that have been filling their positions in multiple divisions under Holy Spirit supervision and alongside angel princes such as Michael, Gabriel, and other angel generals.

We are moving into the era when more angels will be sent from Heaven to assist Christ's heirs than any other period in history. It's time for the assistance of angels partnering with Christ's ekklesia, His New Testament church, at levels never before seen.

At the beginning of 2020, Holy Spirit spoke to me concerning a new-era decade of greater glory and a special Pentecost that was now fully come. It was in its fullness of time. He specifically stated, "My people will move into a new-era Pentecost."

There are three literal Pentecosts that are important to understand in order to discern our times. The first literal Pentecost took place 50 days after the first Passover. Moses led God's people to Mount Sinai, and they camped around the mountain as Moses climbed up it to talk with

God. The Israelites celebrated this with a feast called Shavuot (or Feast of Firstfruits), which the Greeks called Pentecost.

The second literal Pentecost took place in Acts 2, 50 days after Jesus became our Passover Lamb on the cross, when Holy Spirit was poured out on the 120 who had gathered in the upper room. He came to live in believers and to fill them with power from on high so they could be Christ's witnesses.

Holy Spirit actually came. Power from Heaven was poured out and signs, wonders, miracles, and great harvest took place. The second literal Pentecost was magnificently "more" than the other Pentecosts of thanksgiving and remembrance over the past centuries. It was far more, as Holy Spirit actually came, and they were filled with His presence and power.

Holy Spirit is saying to the church today that we are now moving into a third literal Pentecost, far greater than Acts 2, with some new aspects added. This third Pentecost is activating the revelation of God's Word to, and through, His people in deeper ways. We will clearly see the plans and strategies that He will open to us in His Word. This new-era Pentecost will activate harvest, blessings, and power from Heaven. It is one that deploys the ekklesia to function in higher authority and, merged with angel armies under Holy Spirit supervision, to disciple nations. This new-era Pentecost is surging in awesome glory and will overcome the kingdom of darkness, withering the roots and the fruit of hell with overwhelming power from Heaven. This is not a onetime event but a continuous outpouring.

## HOLY SPIRIT,

*Your coming is not an idea, but a reality. When You come, You bring monumental breakthrough and You pour out new measures of Yourself that we've never experienced before. Fill us afresh today. Anoint us with Your power and presence. Show us Your glory! Ready us for this new outpouring, this new Pentecost.*

# BREAKING OUT
# OF CONFINEMENT

> **WE DECREE** Holy Spirit and His angels
> are delivering us from confinement.

The angel armies are now being added in new ways, and at new levels, in this third literal Pentecost. The previous Pentecosts described angelic assistance, but now it will be far greater. Division after division of God's hosts, which have been reserved for our times, are being deployed with us. They partner to assist Christ's Kingdom government to break up, break out, break through, passover, and possess, just as they helped the Israelites break out of Egypt, passover, and possess their promise.

There is a Scripture that points to this in the Exodus. It's been overlooked, but it pictures an amazing promise of new Pentecost:

> *Now the sojourning of the children of Israel, who dwelt in Egypt, was four hundred and thirty years. And it came to pass at the end of the four hundred and thirty years, even the selfsame day it came to pass, that all the hosts of the Lord went out from the land of Egypt* (Exodus 12:40-41 KJV).

The word for *hosts* is the Hebrew word *tsebaah* and it means "a large group of angels" (Strong's H6635). It references the angel hosts, as in the hosts that surround the throne of God. It also references army troops, as in a large division of warriors, and it is the word for angel armies.

A host of people left Egypt with Moses, but so did the heavenly hosts that were assisting His people. It is both the people *and* the angels, and that's why it's worded this way. It's why this verse doesn't just say the people of God left Egypt. When you think about it, why would the angel armies stay? What would be the purpose?

The angels had been assisting and protecting God's people and helping Lord Sabaoth, the Lord of angel armies, release plagues so His people could be free. The angels of the Lord, who were assisting the Israelites to take great wealth out of Egypt, were no longer needed in Egypt. Their assignment had been to assist God's people to break out of 430 years of bondage.

Now, God has led the people out of that bondage, and the angelic hosts serving that God-ordained purpose left as well. The angel armies went along with the people to protect them, to help with provisions, and to one day in the future help Almighty God break them into new lands of promise. This would begin with an amazing breakthrough at Jericho, where the walls were so thick, horse-drawn chariots could ride and patrol on the top of them. Those walls were busted, shattered, and broken up by God's breakthrough angels, and God's people entered supernatural breakthrough.

> *The people of Israel had lived in Egypt for 430 years. In fact, it was on the last day of the 430th year that all the Lord's forces left the land* (Exodus 12:40-41 NLT).

Please note the wording—*all* the forces of the Lord left the land.

LORD,

*As You've done before, You are doing again—You are leading Your people out of bondage and into new land. Thank You that your angelic hosts are assisting Your church now to break up, break out, breakthrough, passover and possess Your promises. I welcome your angels to bring us into the new Pentecost reserved for our times. Come, Holy Spirit!*

# ANGELS AND PROPHETIC DESTINY

> **WE DECREE** insight and revelation
> for our times is accelerating.

Daniel, who was brilliant and on par with Moses and Solomon, is one of the foremost prophets we are still studying to this day. Daniel revealed several essential keys in how he lived and conducted his life that are vital to us for interpreting our own times.

To accurately interpret the era in which he lived, Daniel received insight and understanding through various means. He would study and pray through the meaning behind dreams, visions, and prophetic words. He also explained riddles, which are statements or questions intentionally phrased so as to require ingenuity in ascertaining the answer or meaning. Daniel could solve complex mysteries, which speaks to things that are hidden from the obvious, and he also interpreted angelic visitations and what those angels communicated to him.

Daniel accomplished all these things through Holy Spirit inspiration. Jesus said that Holy Spirit is our helper and teacher in John 14:26. One way in which Holy Spirit assists us is through angels. Hebrews 1:14 (KJV) says, *"Are they not all ministering spirits, sent forth to minister for them who shall be heirs of salvation?"*

We need to understand this, as it is instructive for our times. Thousands of angels had assisted the people of God in getting out of Babylonian captivity. It was not just the archangels, Michael and Gabriel, but also the angel armies they commanded who battled against the prince of Persia—a demon prince—and his demon armies. They were battling in the spirit realm to open up some doors for Daniel in the natural realm.

Daniel referred to some of the angels that he saw as "watchers." Daniel 4:13 and 4:17 tells us very clearly that the watchers were angels, holy ones from Heaven. These angels were sent by Holy Spirit to assist Daniel and the people of God who were in captivity. They were connecting to promises and answers to prayer, battling to open doors, and changing the hearts of kings and the government of his time.

These watchers/holy ones/angels helped Daniel and God's people see a rebellious government sentenced and changed. They saw Jehovah God proclaimed as the ultimate ruler over natural kingdoms. I believe that something very similar is now happening in the spirit and the natural earth realms today.

Daniel, of course, was an Old Testament prophet and he saw all of this angel activity. We are New Testament heirs of God, joint heirs with Christ, and have greater authority than Daniel ever thought about having. A part of our prophetic destiny involves the activation of millions of angels to assist us in this new era decade when the ekklesia becomes the King's mouth. It's not a matter of just a few angels here and there. Rather, it is millions of angels with all kinds of different abilities, callings, and giftings that are watching from everywhere to assist us. They are here to help us activate prophetic destiny, if we will just search it out and find it.

JESUS,
*Thank You for Your Holy Spirit, our Helper and Teacher. Thank You that Holy Spirit works with Your angelic hosts to activate our prophetic destinies and bring answers to prayer. Like Daniel, please anoint us with insight to understand our times and partner with Your Holy Spirit and Your angelic hosts to see Your Kingdom established upon the earth.*

# THE AID OF GOD'S CAVALRY DIVISION

**WE DECREE** God's cavalry will
assist us to win great victories.

Second Kings 6:17 tells us that the prophet Elisha and his servant saw an innumerable number of angels in chariots of fire, and they also saw fire spirit horses. These were seen, not in the natural, but in the spirit, which doesn't make them any less real. In fact, the Scriptures teach that the spirit realm is *more* real than the natural realm, because the spirit realm is eternal while the natural realm is temporary. So please understand that the spirit horses and chariots were real. It was God's way, in Second Kings, of showing man that He has the most powerful army that there is, and it's real.

He has a cavalry that's available to come to His people's aid, to fight for and with them, and to protect them. They are powerful enough to accomplish the mission against any activities of hell, or any activity in the natural realm, as when Elisha's servant had exclaimed that they were surrounded by the Syrian armies. When Elisha told him, "Don't worry... there are more on our side than on their side," the servant's eyes were opened and he saw God's awesome army.

We have powerful angels in God's cavalry division that are available to us and are now being emphasized by the Holy Spirit. This mighty division of angels is here today to assist the heirs and the ekklesia of Christ Jesus. If God chose to use this division of angels, how much more important is it for us to be assisted by them as well. They are here and will hearken to the voice of our decrees made in the name of King Jesus. This angel division has not stopped working; it worked with God in

Heaven and it works with us on earth. There are simply times when, in spiritual conflict on earth, we must have the assistance of this mighty cavalry coming to our aid. It is available and one of the greatest benefits Holy Spirit is bringing to assist the glorious ekklesia Jesus is building.

I believe we are now moving into an era when angel armies, activated by Holy Spirit, will bring to pass the decrees of faith of the ekklesia, helping bring to pass the strategies of Holy Spirit on the earth. The greatest decade ever planned by Holy Spirit is now unfolding before us and we're going to see more angel activity and more divisions of angels released to assist than in any other decade in all of church or world history.

The ekklesia of King Jesus will experience the backing of Heaven's cavalry. They are here to assist God's heirs—the joint heirs with Christ—and they are going to do exactly that. Hell will find itself facing an awesome remnant warrior church army, and it will also find itself facing the chariots of fire that Heaven is activating on the earth. And, just as Elisha's servant saw, there are more of Heaven's elite warriors with us than those that are against us.

## GOD,

*Thank You that there are always more on our side. Thank You that Heaven's calvary is working on behalf of the church to see King Jesus get His full reward. Open our eyes to see Your angelic armies working alongside of us. Fill our mouths with Your decrees so that Your elite warriors may be mobilized on the earth!*

# Angels of Revelation and Enlightenment

> **WE DECREE** the watcher angels will communicate revelation and enlightenment to us. We decree the portals are open for angels to ascend and descend.

Angels of enlightenment, or revelation angels, explained matters to people in biblical times, such as Daniel, Abraham, Joshua, Jeremiah, Zechariah, Paul, Peter, and John, to name a few. These angels assisted Holy Spirit in downloading information to John in his book called the Revelation.

These highly trained angels are here right now, and in this new-era decade Holy Spirit is going to use them to activate revelation, enlightenment, instructions, and strategies, just as He did in the Old and New Testaments. They are going to be made available to us at higher levels, connecting the ekklesia— the government Kingdom of God—to vital information that is beyond the natural realm of understanding.

As heirs, we have a right to special information that angels can connect us to. We have got to start opening up to spiritual resources that we have not yet been taking advantage of. We must come into agreement with Kingdom of God principles, or keys, and ask Holy Spirit to activate angels of enlightenment and revelation to come give us that information so we can function at a much higher and wiser level on this earth.

We have got to normalize what the nominal church and the world consider to be weird Christianity. We need to understand that true Christians and heirs are *supposed* to be assisted by angels. We're *supposed* to be guarded, delivered, strengthened, and connected to resources by them. Angels are *supposed* to assist in battle and set us free. We're *supposed* to be blessed and informed by them. It's in the Bible and we believe it.

It's time to raise the bar and stop living lowered, watered down Christianity and begin living in Bible reality. Yes, angels assist me. Yes, angels sometimes talk to me and give me messages from Heaven. No, I am never alone. Holy Spirit is always with me and so are His angels. What's odd to me are people who see demons everywhere, hearing devils talking to them all the time. It's weird to listen to the devil and his demons. It's a whole lot smarter to listen to Holy Spirit and the real angels of God. Where in the world did we get so far gone that we think listening to angels is weird, and hearing from demons is *not* weird?

We need to declare the portal open for angels of enlightenment to ascend and descend and engage with us, connecting us to supernatural information and understanding, intelligence gathering that we can't do, and secrets, conditions, enemy tactics, and positioning that they are commissioned to communicate to us. This will accelerate a movement that cannot be stopped.

## HOLY SPIRIT,

*I declare today that the portals are open for angels of enlightenment to ascend and descend, engaging with Your church and connecting us to supernatural understanding! Thank You that Your angels love to work alongside of Your people. I come into agreement today with Your principles and I ask You for a fresh anointing of Your wisdom to see Your Kingdom come in my life!*

# WELCOMING THE GREATEST CAVALRY

**WE DECREE** we are entering into God-planned seasons of spiritual whirlwinds. We decree divisions of angel armies are based with, and work with, our apostolic hubs.

When the ekklesia becomes the King's mouth on earth, declaring what He says, forbidding what He says should be forbidden and permitting what He wants permitted, we are going to see the chariots of fire, mighty warriors of Heaven, come to our aid and defense. We will see the King's cavalry engage with us in ways that have not been seen for centuries. We are about to see the weapons of our warfare that have been reserved for an operational ekklesia. Information will be revealed, enabling us to release decrees that need to be decreed. We have entered into the God-planned season of spiritual whirlwinds and chariots of fire in the hands of Heaven's warriors, coming to assist the transition of ministers and ministries and the promotion of servants.

Where is the God of Elijah? Where is the God of Abraham, Isaac, Jacob, Peter, James, John, and the apostle Paul? The world is about to find out where He is! He is in the midst of His glorious ekklesia, just as He said He was going to be, making His stand with them. When He says He is going to have a glorious ekklesia, He means it, and He is moving divisions of angels into place to assist.

Just as Elijah's servant thought, sometimes we think the numbers are too low. But not if you recognize there's a spirit realm with plenty of angelic warriors. As heirs of God and joint heirs with Christ, we are not helpless. We need to discern our times so we can function as Christ defined us. We have not done that yet, but we will, so we can operate in the real authority of the spiritual Kingdom of God, affecting the natural kingdoms of the earth.

Holy Spirit affirmed all these thoughts to me as I was watching a special documentary concerning the great war fighters of the United States who were helping to fight terrorism in Afghanistan. An Afghan general was interviewed and asked if he had a problem with our troops being on their base. He simply replied, "Oh no, not a problem at all. We welcome the greatest war fighters on the earth. We welcome them."

When he said that, I heard Holy Spirit say this to me: "You need to welcome the greatest cavalry to your base. You need to welcome the greatest war fighters, the greatest warriors in the universe, to your apostolic base. If you will, they will guard you from hell's terrorism and protect the awakening and the harvest of the ages that I have assigned to you."

Please know we have awesome, fierce warriors available to share our apostolic and prophetic bases with us. We need to welcome them and release them with decrees of faith that Holy Spirit prompts inside of us.

We also need to welcome the division of angels under Gabriel—the angels of enlightenment, revelation, and communication—to be a part of our apostolic hubs.

Let's activate the assignment of Heaven against hell's strategies. Our strategies will win. Hell's strategies will lose. We decree it in Jesus' name.

## KING JESUS,

*I pray today for Your ekklesia to become Your mouthpiece on the earth, decreeing and declaring Your promises and principles into every situation. As we speak, please anoint our words to bring breakthrough and to activate Your angel armies. I welcome Your angels to come now as Heaven's strategies are being activated on the earth.*

# Mobilizing Angels Through Prayer

> **WE DECREE** the angels of the
> Lord are bringing our prayers to pass.

In the Book of Daniel, Daniel had been praying over the future of his nation and had asked for help and wisdom from God. We are told that God heard Daniel's prayer the very first day that he started praying and had sent one of the most powerful angels, an archangel named Gabriel, with an answer. However, there was spiritual warfare that took place between Heaven and earth in the astrological, or atmospheric, Heaven between Gabriel and a demon prince, the spirit prince of Persia.

This spirit prince of Persia was warring against Gabriel to stop him from getting through to Daniel with the answer to the prayer. The battle lasted for 21 days and was quite intense.

> *While I was pouring out my heart, baring my sins and the sins of my people Israel, praying my life out before my God, interceding for the holy mountain of my God—while I was absorbed in this praying, the humanlike Gabriel, the one I had seen in an earlier vision, approached me, flying in like a bird about the time of evening worship. He stood before me and said, "Daniel, I have come to make things plain to you"* (Daniel 9:20-22 MSG).

Gabriel told Daniel, "I'm here to give you God's answer to your prayer and to help you understand the strategy of the King. You have a good future in store, and I'm going to assist you in understanding it." Clearly, God assigns angels to bring us answers to prayer. They organize around the prayers of the saints to bring them to pass—especially the prayers of an ekklesia over a region.

I believe that's why the kingdom of hell fights corporate prayer so intensely. When the ekklesia gathers in corporate prayer, it mobilizes angels. To change regions or to change a nation often requires angelic assistance, and it's why they have been given to us. Throughout Scripture, we see angels getting people out of trouble in their nations, cities, or in corporate ways, bringing answers to their prayers.

One of the ways in which you can identify whether you are in a brand-new era in the Kingdom is by fresh anointings of Holy Spirit. Everywhere I go, I am seeing new anointings and outpourings of the Holy Spirit. It's not like it was a few years ago; there's something happening in the atmosphere. Second, there is increased angel activity. Angels always assist the new eras and new moves of God. Study this in history and you will see angel activity every time. And third, the prophetic words of the apostles and the prophets will declare it.

All three of those things are happening now in accelerated ways on the earth. I've never seen more Kingdom activity in my entire life; it's as if Heaven has amped up, and we need to amp up with it.

## HOLY SPIRIT,

*I ask today for a fresh grace of intercession to fall upon me. Lead me as I pray, show me how to partner with Your heart for breakthrough. And as Your church prays, may your angels be mobilized. May our regions and nations be changed as the result of Your praying church.*

# THE CHURCH AND GOVERNMENT ANGELS

> **WE DECREE** the government angels are assisting the ekklesia to reign with Christ. We decree the ekklesia is being mantled with greater governing apparel.

At an Appeal to Heaven Conference in Tucson, Arizona, I had preached on the Standing King in the evening, and the next day we were making prayer decrees. After I spoke, I stepped off to the side, and immediately I saw government angels with the purple sashes lined up all the way up one wall, across the back, and down the other side. I had never seen so many angels in one place before.

I said, "Holy Spirit, I've never seen so many government angels," and He replied, *"There are 51 of them, if you want to count."* I asked Him why they were here and He replied, *"They are here representing each state capital and one for Washington, D.C. They're here to receive their assignments."*

I told my brother, Dutch, what I had just seen and heard and we began making decrees. As the name of each state was spoken out, that state's angel would leave.

The prophetic picture of this comes to us in the story of Esther and her uncle, Mordecai. Haman, a wicked government official, had tricked the king into signing an evil decree stating that anyone could kill any Jew that they wanted and confiscate their property. Unbeknownst to the king, Queen Esther and Mordecai were Jews. They went before the king and asked him, "Please, reverse this evil decree," but the king said, "No, I'm not going to do it. If you want the decree rewritten, you do it. I will give you authority to do it, but I won't do it for you." Esther 8 tells us the king then gave Mordecai his signet ring, which meant Mordecai could do business any time, any place, in the name of the king.

We are then told in Esther 8:15 that Mordecai left the king's presence dressed differently, in royal apparel of blue, white, and purple. Additionally, he received the king's signet ring and a crown of gold, which symbolized governing authority. Mordecai was mantled with the king's delegated authority to reign, govern, change laws, and make new laws.

Please hear what the Holy Spirit is saying about this new era: a fresh move of governing authority is now being given to the ekklesia. Holy Spirit, the brilliant strategist, is releasing angels to assist that governing authority to come to pass. In this fresh move, angels will aid the saints in ruling and reigning on the earth at higher levels than have ever taken place in the Kingdom of God.

Just as Mordecai looked different when he came out from the king's presence, so the ekklesia is going to look different in this new era. God is clothing us with governing apparel and a maturing of executive authority is going to be seen in believers everywhere.

## GOD,

*Thank You that You are clothing Your ekklesia with new, governmental authority. Like Mordecai, please anoint us with Your delegated authority to reign in our homes, regions and nations and see Your Kingdom come. Thank You that Your angels are now assisting us to rule with You at higher levels.*

# RISE AND RULE

> **WE DECREE** the ekklesia will rise
> and rule as intended.

In my study on angels, I began to understand that there are millions of awakening angels that are here to assist a new outpouring of Holy Spirit. I believe these are some of the same angels that were mentioned assisting Holy Spirit in Acts 2. There are no angel graveyards; angels don't die. They are still here, partnering with Holy Spirit in new moves, or campaigns, on the earth. A portion of every outpouring down through history has been reserved for now.

As I was praying and preparing for service one Sunday, I began to feel a prophetic anointing stirring inside of me. I continued praying in the spirit for another 20 minutes or so, when Holy Spirit began showing me a vision.

In this vision, I saw a huge funnel, like the type that's used to pour oil into a car's engine, with a big bowl at one end and a stem at the other end. The bowl of the funnel was actually like a television screen and I began to see various scenes scrolling around the sides of it. There were scenes, one after another, of events down through the ages, including the Book of Acts, church history and events, great revivals and prayer meetings, revivalists and evangelists, and other great movements of history. It was as if I was watching a movie. After a while, the scenes began to circle further down into the funnel bowl and were being squeezed into the narrow stem at the bottom, running out into our times.

Not wanting to surmise the meaning, I asked, "Holy Spirit, what are You showing me?" He answered, "I'm pouring the anointings and the streams of Christ's Kingdom throughout the ages into the new era we've prepared for the glorious ekklesia."

I then asked, "What am I to do with this?" He stated, "You are to declare that it is now connected to its moment. The synergy and convergence of the ages have begun. The anointings and outpourings have begun. The activation of prophetic words has begun. Pray it, decree it, prophesy it, guard it. Steward its activation into your times."

His words then became like a prophecy: "For you have entered a fullness of time and are entering the second apostolic age, an era of signs, wonders and miracles." This was the second time Holy Spirit talked to me about the second apostolic age.

"It is the era," said the Lord, "when the ekklesia sits on the throne of their regions and influences the natural realms of earth through the spiritual Kingdom. Watch the ekklesia rise, for it shall surely rise. It is purposed. It shall be so. It will rise and it will rule as intended, for it has now connected to its moment. Watch the change and the changes. Align with Heaven and you will see it on earth. Align with Heaven and activate the rapid change. Speak your agreement. Speak to the fog. Command it to lift and you will see the new era."

## LORD JESUS,

*I pray today in alignment with Your prophetic promises—the synergy of the ages has begun! May Your awakening angels come now, activating Your ekklesia to take their rightful place on the thrones of our regions. May Your angels strengthen us to rise as we are anointed with what Your Kingdom has seen through ages past.*

# REVIVAL THAT CHANGES A NATION

**WE DECREE** America shall be saved.
We decree bend us, bend us, bend us.

Holy Spirit is saying to us, "Remember the Welsh Revival. Pick up the mantle of the Welsh Revival." Holy Spirit has repeatedly spoken to me that the revival in America will be like the Welsh Revival.

Evan Roberts was a young man who worked in the coal mines; he was also a blacksmith. Today, we would define him as a millennial. Roberts spent hours praying and reading his Bible, often all night long. He was the youth pastor at his church and also taught Sunday school. At the age of 26, after praying and seeking the Lord for days, he felt led to go to a missions conference led by Evangelist Seth Joshua. At the end of the meeting, the evangelist prayed a prayer and one particular line was, "Lord, bend us," which was a phrase used in those times for holiness. It's not really used in that way today. In other words, "Bend us to follow You, Lord. Make our hearts pliable. Soften us, Lord. Bend us into who we need to be. Bend my life so it is usable, Lord. Shape us."

As Seth Joshua prayed, "Bend us, Lord," people in the congregation began to spontaneously pray out loud. Evan Roberts writes of that moment:

> When others prayed I felt a living force come into my bosom. It held my breath, and my legs shivered. ...The living force grew and grew, and I was almost bursting. ...I cried, "Bend me! Bend me! Bend us!" What bent me was God commending His Love...and I wept. Henceforth the

salvation of souls became the burden of my heart. From that time I was on fire with a desire to go through all Wales.

And the young man did just that. Conservative estimates are that over 150,000 gave their hearts to Christ. Bars closed and crime was practically nonexistent. The police actually said they had little to do besides managing the crowds who were going to a revival or church meeting. The people were so joyful, and they sang so much that the revival simply became known as the "Singing Revival."

Thousands of coal miners were saved, many of whom were hardcore sinners. These coal miners now loved to sing while they worked. It was said the mules that carted off the coal had to be retrained because they had been trained by these hard miners to follow the command of curse words; they didn't understand kind words.

The coal mine had large air shafts running hundreds of feet down into the earth all over the Welsh hillsides. People would bring chairs and sit around those air shafts, listening for hours to the reverberating songs and hymns echoing up from the bowels of the earth, from men who were now saved. The songs would travel down the line as various men joined in, singing for so long that all around the hillside you could hear the songs coming up from the earth. No one sings quite like the Welsh; theirs is an accent that gets into your soul. It is so hard to imagine this, but the countryside literally echoed with praise and worship wafting up from the ground. All of Wales was changed, and then the nations around them began to change.

## HOLY SPIRIT,

*What You ignited in Evan Roberts, ignite in me. What You poured out on Wales, pour out on my region. What You've done before, do again. Bend us, Lord. Soften us, Holy Spirit. Shape us, Jesus. I yield to You afresh today. Send revival to my home and my nation!*

# ANGELS OF AWAKENING

**WE DECREE** the synergy and convergence of the ages has begun. We decree the war eagles are rising.

Holy Spirit has released awakening angels to connect us to the anointings of previous revivals. They are also connecting us to the great awakening that is planned for our times. They are connecting us to prophetic words, visions, and dreams. The Third Great Awakening has begun.

Recently, we received another dream from Gina Gholston.

"I dreamed I was on the grounds of the Red River Meeting House in Russellville, Kentucky. I had gone through the gate and started walking up the driveway toward the Meeting House. In front of me, in the dip as you go up to the building, I noticed that there were close to 100 bald eagles standing on the ground. I was captivated by the sight of all the eagles.

"Then, hearing a noise behind me, I turned and saw one of those older well drilling rigs coming through the gate toward the meeting house. It stopped about halfway up the driveway and backed up toward the meeting house, stopping under the walnut trees. Then, those on the truck began drilling, and no sooner had the bit been set when, whoosh—the water came gushing out in massive amounts. In the dream I thought, 'This looks like Old Faithful.'

"I have seen that geyser and this made me think of that, only this was much larger in the dream. I was thinking about how Old Faithful is very predictable and that it gushes forth in a rhythm of time. Then, I heard an audible voice speaking about the geyser in front of me that was now gushing forth, and it said, 'It is set on the rhythm of Heaven's time clock. It's time.'

"In this dream I understood that statement to mean that it's blown before. A gushing move of the Holy Spirit has blown before, but it's set for another, greater gush this time. Next, I saw two hands come down and clap once. The clap made a very loud sound, and when it came it was a signal to the eagles. When they heard the clap, the eagles rose up, hovering, ready to fly. They weren't scared by the noise of the clap or by the spraying of the water. They all just simultaneously rose up and calmly hovered.

"When they started rising up, I saw that each eagle carried arrows in one talon and rolled up papers in the other talon. As they rose up, hovering, I heard the voice say, 'Rapid eye movement. My seers are on the move. My watchers are on the move.'

"As soon as I heard those words, the eagles flew off in every direction, each heading purposefully in the direction they were sent, carrying out their own assignments. As they left the Red River Meeting House, they each flew through the gushing water, getting the water on them and carrying it with them. The water never dried off of them. Wherever they went as they flew, the water would fall off of them like a rain shower onto the dry ground they were flying over...."

## HOLY SPIRIT,

*Thank You that You are now releasing angels of awakening that are connecting Your ekklesia to anointings of past revivals. Dispatch Your war eagles to bring a fresh baptism of Your Spirit into every part of the earth. What You poured out at the Red River Meeting House, pour out today. Ignite a fire in our souls to see revival sweep across our nation!*

# THE CONVERGENCE
# OF REVIVALS

**WE DECREE** the anointings on the Cane Ridge, Azusa Street, and the Welsh Revivals will now synergize into our times. We decree it is time for the gusher.

Gina's dream continues:

"The water was still gushing and I, too, was soaked with it. I went into the Meeting House, which was set up like a command center. There were perhaps seven drafting tables set up, with architects sitting at them, drawing up blueprints or plans. People were coming in one right after the other, soaked in the water from the gusher. Each person would approach one of the architects who were drawing up the blueprints, who would then tear off a blueprint, roll it up, and hand to the person.

"It's hard to explain, but immediately after rolling up one blueprint, the architects would quickly have another one drawn, which they would roll up and hand off to the next person in line. I was amazed at the speed of the architects in their work. They were drawing, rolling, and handing—this was happening over and over, very, very quickly.

"Then I noticed there were pipes built into the walls of the Red River Meeting House going out in every direction...When the people received those blueprints, the architects would point them in the direction of a certain pipe. They would get in that pipe and be sent where they needed to go with those blueprints, those plans.

"In the dream, I thought this process was similar to sending emails. I thought of fiber optics. I knew that, just like it was with an email, these people were getting into the pipes and were being sent along with the blueprints, strategies, plans, and revelations. Wherever in the world they were sent, as soon as they got in the pipe, whoosh—they instantly arrived at their destination, soaked with the water that had sprayed on them from the gushing well, raining off of them like it did with the eagles...

"I was then lifted up and could see a drawing of a line connecting Cane Ridge, Kentucky and the Red River Meeting House, and going out from Cane Ridge were other lines, with one line from each of them going to Azusa. As I was lifted up high above the nation, I saw that these lines formed the shape of a spearhead. From the line that was drawn between Cane Ridge and Red River was another line and I knew that this line was coming from the nation of Wales.

"It was a drawing depicting that all four of these places—Cane Ridge, Red River Meeting House, Azusa, and Wales—were all connecting, and that what I saw happening at Red River was simultaneously happening in all the other places. I knew I was being shown that the culmination of all those past moves of God were now being brought together to spearhead another greater and more powerful move of God in our times. They were converging."

Hear what Holy Spirit is saying: "It's time for the gusher! It's time for old healing wells and revival wells to be uncapped. Awakening angels are connecting us to Holy Spirit strategies with past streams of revival and past anointings that are now activating in our times."

New streams for our times are flowing and new anointings are synergizing together. It is time to see all of this; it's time for our future to change. A move of God is beginning that cannot be stopped.

## LORD JESUS,

*Uncap the wells of revivals past! Please fill Your church with a hunger for a new outpouring of Your Spirit. As Cane Ridge, Red River Meeting House, Azusa and Wales impacted the earth, may this new move of Your presence impact the world. I posture my heart for this revival and declare that I am ready for the gusher!*

# A Fresh Breath

**WE DECREE** new breath is entering God's people and a great army is rising.

*God grabbed me. God's Spirit took me up and set me down in the middle of an open plain strewn with bones. He led me around and among them—a lot of bones! There were bones all over the plain— dry bones, bleached by the sun.*

*He said to me, "Son of man, can these bones live?" I said, "Master God, only you know that." He said to me, "Prophesy over these bones: 'Dry bones, listen to the Message of God!'" God, the Master, told the dry bones, "Watch this: I'm bringing the breath of life to you and you'll come to life. I'll attach sinews to you, put meat on your bones, cover you with skin, and breathe life into you. You'll come alive and you'll realize that I am God!" I prophesied just as I'd been commanded. As I prophesied, there was a sound and, oh, rustling! The bones moved and came together, bone to bone. I kept watching. Sinews formed, then muscles on the bones, then skin stretched over them. But they had no breath in them.*

*He said to me, "Prophesy to the breath. Prophesy, son of man. Tell the breath, 'God, the Master, says, Come from the four winds. Come, breath. Breathe on these slain bodies. Breathe life!'" So I prophesied, just as he commanded me. The breath entered them and they came alive! They stood up on their feet, a huge army* (Ezekiel 37:1-10 MSG).

In this passage in Ezekiel, we see a prophetic vision and hear a prophetic word. A "new breath" is entering God's people and resurrection life will cause them to come together and stand as a great army. I began to picture sails, as on a ship, rising into Holy Spirit winds. A knowing in my spirit came—winds were going to blow the church from the doldrums into fresh waters and new ports of blessing. Holy Spirit was bringing fresh breath to "life" His body; it would no longer be a disconnected skeleton. The graves would be opened and the church would come to life.

I am hearing the sound of rattling as bones are coming together, as ligaments and muscles are being formed. I hear the sound of wind resuscitating, invigorating, and "life-ing" God's people. Christ is not returning for a dead bride, dead church, or a demoralized, frightened army. He's coming for a glorious church without spot or wrinkle, one that will begin to disciple nations.

There is a cure for deadness. It's called "resurrection" and our King has it mastered. I don't hear funeral dirges, as some are proclaiming. I'm not hearing the bugle playing taps. I hear the sound of reveille. I hear resurrection life being breathed from the throne room.

Our King, along with Holy Spirit and His strategies, assisted by millions of angels, is working now to breathe life into the true church. It is accelerating into a spectacular movement confirmed by signs, wonders, miracles, healings, breakthrough, and harvest. A billion-soul revival is coming and a Kingdom move of God, greater than most have ever thought possible, has begun.

### LORD JESUS,

*Thank You that You are the Resurrection and the Life. Thank You that You are breathing fresh breath into Your church. I welcome Your Holy Spirit and Your angels to bring resurrection power into Your church, igniting new signs and wonders and sparking an abundant harvest of souls. As You breathe on us, Your army is coming back to life!*

# THE RELEASE OF RE-VIVE-ALL ANGELS

> **WE DECREE** God's supernatural strength is being breathed into His people. We decree re-vive-all angels are assisting Holy Spirit in breathing fresh life into God's people.

On February 14, 2019, I began to see in the spirit realm extremely strong winds blowing from the four corners of the earth. Holy Spirit is the *ruwach* of God. He's the Breath Spirit that entered the lifeless skeletons, causing them to come alive (Ezekiel 37).

In my vision, Holy Spirit was blowing life from all directions and I could see thousands of angels riding upon those four winds. I began to pray, "God, what are You showing me? Give me understanding." In my spirit, I heard Holy Spirit say, "This is a division of angels now being released for the new days."

Re-vive-all angels are being deployed on Holy Spirit winds. They are being activated and are riding Breath Spirit's wind into all the earth. They are assisting Holy Spirit's strategy to re-vive-all the remnant in various capacities.

- They assist in overcoming helplessness and despair.
- They assist in ending a season of hope deferred.
- They aid in helping to end lengthy battles.
- They help bring God's supernatural strength to His people.
- They assist in firing up, encouraging, invigorating, and breathing resurrection life.

- They revive-them-all to stand on their feet, staking their place in the King's victorious army.
- They assist in reviving the remnant to take their place in the glorious church, for which the King is returning.

Holy Spirit is answering our prayers by deploying millions of angels to revive us, to reinvigorate the bride and fill their lamps with oil. The outpouring is a replenishing one, so the bride can take all she needs—there will be plenty more. The fresh winds of revival are blowing. I believe these revival angels are assisting Holy Spirit in the times of refreshing referred to in Acts 3:20.

Many of us have been through what seem to be times of desert heat, bleaching us to the bone. We've endured hot times when we've felt very dry, when it seemed our hope was gone and there was nothing left. We've seen our visions strewn about and disconnected in the desert valleys. We've been picked clean by opportunistic demon vultures, while satanic wolves have scattered our bones every which way. But Breath Spirit says the bones can live. Breath Spirit says, "Watch this. I'm bringing the breath of life to you and you'll come to life."

On the day of Pentecost in Acts 2, a small remnant of 120 believers sat in an upper room in Jerusalem. Life burst forth and transformation came as God's breath blew upon them and resurrection surged into a hopeless, fearful body of people. Disciples, buried by difficult situations and loss, came alive. Widows, orphans, and the poor, who had been entombed in societal grief and governmental domination by the Roman Empire, were revived.

Re-vive-all angels are assisting Holy Spirit in breathing fresh life into God's people. They are aiding Holy Spirit strategy in strengthening and encouraging the remnant. No matter what the circumstance, no matter your condition, you can be revived.

## HOLY SPIRIT,

*I welcome Your re-vive-all-angels! May Your breath come from Heaven, bringing fresh life into Your sons and daughters. Give us understanding as to what You are doing and how You are moving, so that we may partner with You. Thank You that no matter the circumstance, there is always hope for revival with You.*

# REVIVING THE REMNANT

| **WE DECREE** a billion soul revival is coming. |

During the Second Great Awakening in the 1800s that was led by Charles Finney, Dwight L. Moody, Billy Sunday, and many others, there were several songs featured in the revivals that had been written by Fanny J. Crosby. Despite being totally blind, Fanny wrote over 8,000 songs during her lifetime.

Due to Fanny's blindness, she had to memorize her 8,000 songs. She also memorized much of the Scripture and stories of the Bible.

One day, Fanny was invited to go to a prison in Manhattan to sing several of her songs and to share from the Scriptures she had memorized. One of the stories that she told is found in Matthew 20:29-34, about two blind beggars who were sitting by the road outside of Jericho. They heard that Jesus was passing by and started calling and shouting out, "Have mercy on us! Have mercy, Lord. Jesus, have mercy on us."

The crowds around Jesus told the beggars, "Be quiet! Jesus has people to call on; He has people to see. Be quiet." But the two beggars just pleaded even louder, "Jesus, have mercy on us. Don't pass us by."

Of course, Jesus didn't pass them by. He stopped and healed their blindness.

Fanny Crosby, being herself blind, told that story with such passion and anointing and so vividly that men up and down the jail cells began to call out, "Jesus, don't pass us by. Do not pass me by."

One man in particular, in a pleading, sobbing, wailing voice, shouted out very loudly, "Please, Jesus, do not pass me by."

On her way home that night from the Manhattan prison, Fanny said she couldn't get the man's desperate pleading out of her mind, so she wrote a song about it that very night, with his wailings echoing in her ears. It would be the song that actually made her famous. It was sung almost every night in the London revivals of the Second Great Awakening, and many times, people attending the revivals would shout out, "Jesus, please! Don't pass me by!"

The writers of those old revival songs meant for them to be felt.

The Appalachian people stewarded those old revival songs, along with the black churches of America. The black churches kept the revival spirit in many of their songs. Their choirs of today reflect that spirit, and we need the wind on it, blowing revival through the land again. True revival is not a white revival. It's black, red, yellow, brown, and white—of every kindred, tribe, and tongue. We need the synergy of all the races, and we need the synergy of all the revival anointings. We need to plead for revival the way we used to. We need a gusher.

There are so many who are in prisons, perhaps not a natural prison but those of other makings, and they're calling out, "Jesus, don't pass me by."

All over the earth, a division of re-vive-all angels is now activated to assist Holy Spirit in this new Pentecost era in reviving the remnant warriors. Re-vive-all angels are moving under Holy Spirit leadership for the greatest revival in history.

GOD,
*Thank You for the leadership of Your Holy Spirit, bringing about the greatest revival the world has ever seen. I cry out to You in fresh surrender, "Don't pass me by!" Fill me with Your glorious presence. I plead with You to synergize the races, the revival anointings, the generations. Pour out revival on us, Lord!*

# ANGELS AND
# FULFILLED DESTINY

> **WE DECREE** angels are helping us understand
> the strategy of King Jesus for our future. We
> decree angels are organizing around the prayers
> of God's people, helping to bring them to pass.

*"I don't think the way you think. The way you work isn't the
way I work." God's Decree. "For as the sky soars high above
earth, so the way I work surpasses the way you work, and the
way I think is beyond the way you think. Just as rain and snow
descend from the skies and don't go back until they've watered
the earth, doing their work of making things grow and blos-
som, producing seed for farmers and food for the hungry,
so will the words that come out of my mouth not come back
empty-handed. They'll do the work I sent them to do, they'll
complete the assignment I gave them"* (Isaiah 55:8-11 MSG).

Notice that God's prophetic words, dreams, and visions to us have
assignments that He has breathed upon them and they are empowered
to do what He says when His people stand in faith for them. Prophetic
words are connecting to their moment, corporately and individually.
It is true for your life, your family, your business, vocation, and ministry; it is across the board. God's promises will connect to their moment.

In Daniel 9, we see this principle of prophetic words intersecting
with their moment as prophetic prayers, strategies, and instructions
concerning a new era play out in an extremely dramatic way. It's a prayer
of Daniel that is instructive as well as fascinating. This is a prayer that
absolutely changed history by changing a nation. It activated prophetic

promises and caused Heaven to respond, and it caused the release of angel princes and their armies from Heaven.

We must understand that the Bible is not only a history of what has happened but is also instructive for today. We are in Holy Spirit times, just like Daniel or any of the prophets or apostles. They were not a different class of people than we are. They were in a spiritual realm that is available to us, as well. They were God's people, just as we are. Respect them, absolutely, but do not deify them. As born-again ones, we, too, are in Holy Spirit times of God-appointed, powerful angelic assistance. We can, and we should, experience supernatural Kingdom of God activity. Actually, because of a new covenant and the baptism of the Holy Spirit, we should experience it even more so.

Remember, Daniel was praying for wisdom concerning his nation and the future. God heard his prayer the first day he started praying and sent the angel, Gabriel, with the answer to that prayer. Gabriel said, "I'm here to help you understand the strategy that the King has for your future. There is a future and it is good. I'm here to assist and answer your prayers."

Clearly, God assigns angels to answer prayers. They organize around the prayers of God's people, helping to bring them to pass— especially the prayers of an ekklesia for a region or nation. Angels engage in spiritual warfare against hell's principalities and powers. They help us battle to bind princes that are trying to stop prayer, prophetic words, or the strategies of God for a new era.

### LORD,

*Today I remind myself that Your angels mobilize at the prayers of the saints. So, today I pray with fresh fervor, believing that with my intercession Your angelic armies are dispatched on assignment—into my family, region and nation. Thank You that prophetic promises and prayers are now intersecting with their moments of fulfillment. May You be glorified!*

# ANGELIC ASSISTANCE FOR SUPERNATURAL HEALING

> **WE DECREE** our emotions, minds, and souls are free, in Jesus' name. We decree accumulated grief is being removed from the body of Christ.

Not all healing is physical, there are also emotional healings and healings of the soul and the mind. My daughter, Rachel, and her husband, Mark, have adopted two children with special needs from China—Lily and Jaidin. They brought Lily home from China when she was 14 months old, shortly before Christmas.

Carol and I consider it our job to spoil the kids at Christmas, showering them with lots of presents. Of course, Lily had never opened Christmas presents before. Her older sister, Maddie, who was seven, had opened lots of them and was frantically opening them at our house on Christmas Eve. But Lily was just sitting and watching, not really knowing what to do. Maddie began picking things out around the house that we already owned to give us for Christmas. She wrapped them, using gobs of tape, and brought them to us to open.

Lily, seeing this, began to play with the tape, instead of opening presents. I was watching all of this intently. When she was done playing with the tape, she tried to set it down but of course the tape stuck to her hand. She then reached over with her other hand and grabbed the tape and tried to set it down with that hand but again the tape stuck to her hand. She did this several times, growing increasingly more frustrated to the point of tears, not being able to get rid of the tape. Seeing her frustration, I took the tape away and we taught her how to open presents. She became a pro instantly.

I woke up in the middle of the night with God speaking to me about accumulated grief. I had never thought about the concept of grief accumulating, but the more I thought about it the more I realized it does happen. The older you get, the more grief in life seems to accumulate. This happens, that happens, and you think you've laid it down but really it's still sticking to the soul and you need someone bigger than you to come along and take it away.

Thankfully, the promise of our great Lord Jesus is that He came to take away grief that accumulates—the divorce, the loss of a loved one, the bankruptcy, the broken relationship. These things can accumulate in our lives, but Jesus comes to unwrap our soul and set us free, healing our emotions, feelings, and minds.

Many today need to be healed in their souls. They're walking around with taped hearts that only Jesus can set free. Thankfully, these divisions of angels that assist with healings and miracles are opening the old healing wells. They are also opening new wells of healings and miracles.

Angels are assisting Holy Spirit to activate the King's anointing to heal, established through the stripes on Jesus' back, at levels the world has never seen before. You will see miracles accelerate. You will see healing accelerate in the physical realm, and you will see dramatic healings of the soul.

**JESUS,**

*Thank You for what You paid for on the cross—for my salvation and my healing. I believe today that by Your stripes I am healed—body, soul and spirit. I invite You to search me and bind up any broken places. May Your healing presence minister to Your church in new ways, bringing restoration and resurrection.*

# UNCAPPING OLD HEALING WELLS

**WE DECREE** healings and miracles are accelerating, in Jesus' name. We decree the world is a pool of Bethesda; angels of healing and miracles are stirring the waters.

The angel divisions of healings and miracles are activating for our times. At the beginning of 2013, I began to have a recurring vision. In the vision, I saw land oil pumps, like you see in the countryside, pumping oil. The lever on these pumps goes up and down, up and down, over and over. However, in my vision, it wasn't a lever doing the pumping—it was an angel. After seeing this vision several times, Holy Spirit spoke to me, saying, "These are angels of healings and miracles. They are pumping the old healing wells and opening new ones."

My father was a healing evangelist and I have been around healing evangelists all my life. I have seen so many miraculous healings. No one could ever tell me miracles aren't real; I've seen them with my own eyes.

When my brother, Dutch, and I were about 12 and 13 years old, we were the "catchers" at the altar. Part of our assignment was to clean up the cancers that were left on the floor after people were healed.

I saw so many miracles, it was ingrained into me that God can do anything. I would believe that anyway, because it's God's Word, but it's at a different level for me because I truly saw miracles take place. At one point, when my dad was pastoring a little church of about 30 to 45 people, he and other local pastors would get together and have a summer revival. They would pray for the sick and, again, Dutch and I would be the "catchers" at the meetings.

One time we were at a small church in Hamilton, Ohio and there were around 40 people in attendance. At this particular meeting, something happened I will never forget as long as I live. A man in a wheelchair was pushed up to the front row where we were sitting. He was completely twisted up, like a pretzel. Three of the local preachers gathered around him, praying in the spirit, and I could hear bones begin to pop, like when a chiropractor works on you. That man began to unwind in his chair and then jumped up onto his feet. He was totally healed, and I will never forget watching that take place.

The Holy Spirit is activating angels to uncap the old healing wells.

*For an angel of God went down at a certain time into the pool and stirred up the water; then whoever stepped in first, after the stirring of the water, was made well of whatever disease he had* (John 5:4 NKJV).

These angels are still stirring the waters. We have moved into this new era, a season when angels are uncapping old healing wells and opening new ones, and when miracles are going to accelerate.

## HOLY SPIRIT,

*Thank You that Your angels are stirring the waters of healing across the earth. Thank You that old healing wells are being uncapped and released afresh in this day and hour. I pray for Your encouragement to flood the church, releasing new expectation for the miraculous. We welcome Your angels of healing and miracles!*

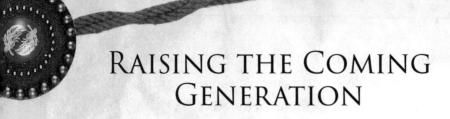

# RAISING THE COMING GENERATION

| **WE DECREE** the magnificent communicators are rising. |

I was awakened in the middle of the night by someone shouting out, "Naphtali!" Carol was asleep, so I wasn't sure who could be doing the yelling. I drifted back to sleep and, once again, I heard "Naphtali!" It still wasn't clicking, but then I heard it a third time, and it sounded as if it was in surround sound. It didn't seem to be coming from downstairs or another room. It was a word that surrounded me: "Naphtali!" and I bolted upright in bed. It sounded as though it could be a Hebrew word, but I didn't recognize it at the time, because I was thinking it was a word for something—perhaps an object— and not someone's name.

Naphtali was a son of Jacob through Rachel's maid, Bilhah. The name *Naphtali* means "my wrestling" or "to twine, twist, or tie up." It also means "to struggle, or a torturous, gut-wrenching type wrestling." Wrestling concerning barrenness and a new generation of children was what this was about.

For the past two decades or so, there has been a wrestling to birth the new movement of the apostolic and the prophetic. There has been a great season of barrenness. It has been a torturous wrestling and gut-wrenching at times. Because it was not accepted well, the warfare against it was very difficult. However, Holy Spirit has brought us to a place of a new birthing and a new move of God. You can feel it rising all over the world. This movement is about birthing new sons and daughters in the Kingdom of God.

Before Jacob died, he called his 12 sons in and blessed them. He declared, "Naphtali is a deer let loose. He giveth goodly words producing magnificent fawns." The Hebrew commentaries tell us that this is referencing the poetic and the speaking characteristics of the tribe of Naphtali. They were great communicators.

The meaning of the phrase is dual in the Hebrew language. It means "producing lovely fawns," which would represent new births. It also carries the concept of producing lovely words, meaning communication is good and clear to produce magnificent fawns.

A fawn, which is a young deer in its first year, represents the coming generation. I began to hear the Lord say it was time to produce magnificent fawns, or communicators, for the Kingdom of God. Like the tribe of Naphtali, we are to produce a coming generation of excellent communicators.

I called a special meeting one evening of those who could further strategize with me concerning what this word, *Naphtali*, was all about. We met upstairs in our church's conference room and spent several hours praying, strategizing, and talking about the meaning and application of this word.

As we prepared to leave at the end of the evening, we looked out of the conference room window, and right beneath it were two fawns with white spots on their back. For as many years as we have been in that location, I had never seen anything like that. What are the chances that on the night we came together and strategized about what to do concerning the magnificent fawns, that two actual fawns would show up under that window? Obviously, it was a confirmation from the Lord that we were to raise the coming generation to be excellent communicators.

## LORD JESUS,

*I bless this coming generation to be all that You intended for them to be! Thank You that this is a season of new birth and You are releasing a fresh grace to communicate effectively. You are birthing new sons and daughters across the world who communicate with fresh authority. I bless their words to bring Kingdom impact in every area of society.*

# ANGELS OF HARVEST

**WE DECREE** evangelism and harvest angels are assisting Holy Spirit and the true ekklesia to reap the billion soul harvest.

*The harvest is the end of the age, and the reapers are the angels* (Matthew 13:39 NKJV).

Jesus said a sign of the end times and His coming would be angels becoming reapers. Two angels are assigned to every person at birth. Their assignment is to pull out the destiny God has planned for them. Before you were ever born, God sat down and wrote your thesis—why He created you. Your two angels are briefed on that and they work to bring it out of you. You may rebel against that destiny, but the angels are not going to stop trying until you die. Evangelism angels help to draw destiny out of people and, of most importance, they draw you to Christ. You must be born again.

Millions of prodigals are about to come home. Many of them were raised in church and they know their Bible. We need to get them home and plugged in. I am convinced some of the greatest apostles, pastors, and ministers in this new era are prodigals who are returning back to the church.

Brand-new, born-again ones are coming in. It's harvest time and evangelism angels are assisting in the harvest of new souls coming into the Kingdom of God.

The fivefold ministry office of an evangelist will be restored and connected to apostolic hubs. This office has to function and we need present-day "Billy Grahams" to come forth. The potential is unlimited and what we are about to see take place in the body of Christ is incredible.

The word *evangelism* has *angel* right in the middle of it. In the Bible, angels are God's messengers, the bearers of the good news of the Gospel. The word *Gospel* is the Greek word *euangelion* (which also has the word *angel* in it) and it was used in several different ways:

- *Euangelion* was used to announce the news of a victory.
- *Euangelion* was used to announce the death of an adversary.
- *Euangelion* was used to announce the birth of a son.
- *Euangelion* was used to announce an upcoming wedding.

The word used for *good news* in the New Testament is the word *Gospel*. We have good news, euangelion, to declare and proclaim to the world.

- Good news! There has been a victory. Calvary defeated hell's plan and Jesus has stripped the devil of his power.
- Good news! There has been a death to our adversary. Jesus destroyed principalities, powers, mights, and dominions, making a show of them openly.
- Good news! A son has been born and His name is Jesus. The angel said, "I bring you good tidings of great joy for unto you is born this day a Savior who is Christ the King."
- Good news! We are heading for a wedding. The largest wedding celebration ever will be held in Heaven at the marriage supper of the Lamb.

We are beginning to see revival outbreaks in the land that will now accelerate worldwide.

## HOLY SPIRIT,

*Thank You that You are releasing the Good News in fresh waves across the world. I ask for angels of evangelism to be released in my region and worldwide, bringing in the greatest harvest of souls ever seen. I pray for revival! I pray for the prodigals to come home. Thank You for the great returning that is taking place in Your church!*

# Angel Armies and the New Campaign

> **WE DECREE** Holy Spirit is leading another campaign, greater than Acts 2, for King Jesus.

Multiple divisions of angel armies are now being sent to earth to assist an emerging and strong ekklesia of King Jesus, a church that embraces the opportunity to reign with Him in this life (see Rom. 5:17). Holy Spirit is in charge of this campaign and is now beginning times of refreshing and outpourings of anointings to empower the heirs to function in His Kingdom, as intended. We have now entered a new-era Pentecost, greater than Acts 2, when replenishing anointings, one after the other, wave after wave, will continue to energize the glorious church, as promised.

We have moved into the season when mighty surges of Holy Spirit power will invigorate Christ's Kingdom on the earth. Supernatural activity that has been seen throughout the ages in certain times and seasons will accelerate in full measure. We will now see a people who represent Jesus as He truly is, doing the same works as He did.

The divisions of angel armies are here to assist the people of God in serving that high purpose. I believe it is why, when Holy Spirit began to reveal angel armies to me years ago, one of His first statements was, "I will now lead another campaign on earth for King Jesus. It will be far greater than the one I led in Acts chapter 2 to birth the New Testament church. But this time, I will be bringing far more of the angel armies. The greatest days in church history are not in your past; they are in your present and in your future."

We are moving into the awesome days we've been promised. Holy Spirit is leading the way and divisions of His powerful angel armies are assisting us to accomplish the new campaign here on earth. A global outpouring of Holy Spirit on a functioning spiritual Kingdom around the world is now being poured out.

Holy Spirit spoke to me concerning a new-era decade of greater glory and a special Pentecost that has now fully come:

It is now in its moment. This year, the ekklesia leaves its training and begins deployment. This will be a year of deployment and change for your future. The functioning ekklesia will rise to operate in higher authority and its advance will be rapid. The world will see the deployment of Heaven's Kingdom ekklesia and angel armies. This will suddenly and aggressively be revealed. Strongholds of hell will be broken and iniquitous roots will dry up under its superior power, authority, and administered justice. The withering of hell's kingdom will begin to be seen in indisputable ways. For the heirs of Kingdom authority are being seated in their regional spheres of influence and their angels, along with the divisions of angels assisting them, are aligning with the assigning. You will now see a clear merger; Heaven and earth will merge in unified oneness of purpose to escalate the King's victories, expand His Kingdom, and implement His spiritual Kingdom's government. The merger of the earth realm with the spirit realm will surge in visible function in this new Pentecost era.

## HOLY SPIRIT,

*I welcome this new-era decade of greater glory! Thank You that You are ushering in a fresh Pentecost and Your ekklesia will rise to operate in greater authority than ever before. I bless the new campaign of Your Spirit and welcome the angels of Heaven to accomplish Your Kingdom strategies. Come and have Your way!*

# THE GLORIOUS CHURCH ERA

> **WE DECREE** the purpose and plans for this
> New Era cannot be reversed. It is immutable.

I heard Holy Spirit say, "The purposes and plans for this era have fully come and will not be reversed. It is an immutable decree of King Jesus for His ekklesia."

That was an unusual statement to have heard. Whenever you hear Holy Spirit use unusual phrasing, pay attention, because there's a reason for doing so. The immutable oath of God's promise is talked about in Hebrews 6. It speaks to a decision that is relentlessly determined to be done, based on the nature and character, abilities and reputation of the one who makes the oath. The immutable oath is decreed seven times; it is a complete, full oath. It was said of the one making the oath that they have seven'd themselves.

The Greek word for *immutable* is *ametathetos*, meaning "unchangeable" (Strong's G276). Holy Spirit was saying to me there are aspects of this new era in which King Jesus has seven'd Himself, swearing they will be implemented, they will be done. He is swearing to His own involvement. The King Himself says there are facets in this new season that are unchangeable for His ekklesia—those who are pursuing a higher level and raising the bar to new boundaries and territories He has put before them.

This is the era of the Kingdom of God's ekklesia on the earth, also referred to as the glorious church era. He's returning for a glorious church and it's going to happen sometime, so why couldn't it happen now? This is the season when the glorious church era begins and we enter into the new boundaries that have been set.

Holy Spirit says, "The purposes and the plans have fully come and they will not be reversed." It is an immutable decree of King Jesus for His true ekklesia. This is its "prepared for" moment—the right time, the right era. Our King has sworn both His and His Kingdom's assistance, as well as angelic participation.

This is the decade when the King will make His stand on the earth, assisting us to break through the obstacles of hell and the strongholds of darkness. In this magnificent era, barrier walls will be smashed by the decrees of the King's ekklesia as it begins to aggressively function as He has sworn it will.

The King, the Breaker Himself, will put His ekklesia on His shoulders and run with them. It's not about whether or not *we* can do it; it's about whether or not *He* can do it.

He swears, "I'm going to do it. I'm going to bust up roadblocks, move mountains, and break you through. You're going to be who I say you are, who I have prepared you to be. You are going to do what I've said you will do. I give My oath that the gates of hell will not prevail against My ekklesia. All the powers of hell combined will not overcome you. It's unchangeable; no compromises, mutations, or appeasing doctrines. I stake My reputation on it. It's immutable."

## JESUS,

*You are returning for a glorious Bride. Thank You that Your ekklesia is being strengthened by Your Spirit to move into greater realms of glory. We will rule and reign with You. Thank You that what You have decreed will come to pass. Your word and Your promises are immutable. We ready ourselves for You, King Jesus!*

# THE KEYSTONE
# ANOINTING

**WE DECREE** the keystone has been raised and the support structure for a New Era Pentecost is in place.

The Lord says:

> When My ekklesia decides to raise the bar, I am going to raise the yoke-destroying anointing, as promised. I'll make My stand with you, running before the decrees that you're making in My name. My Kingdom will advance before you. Angels of breakthrough will accompany Me in order to penetrate the territories that you have soaked with My words of promise. They will break up entrenched powers of darkness in both the natural and the spirit realms, and you will break through. My ekklesia's time and era of breakthrough has fully come; you have crossed the line of demarcation. Rise with Me and run, as My true ekklesia, through doors of hope, opportunity, advancement, and breakthrough.

The prophets are calling this decade the roaring 20s. Get ready because the real remnant, the true church, is in for the ride of their lives. There's a determination of our King Jesus that is going to be seen in this decade. He knows how to set His face like a flint and He is doing that now, in our times. He has fire in His eyes and a sword in His hand.

As I was praying about all of this, I said, "Holy Spirit, tell me about this season. Talk to me about this period of time." I heard this statement: "The keystone is being raised into place." That was not what I was expecting to hear.

The keystone is a stone at the top of a crown or an arch that locks all the other pieces together in a building. It's the stabilizing stone on which the beams lean against, to hold them in place. The weight of the beams leaning against the keystone holds it all in position. A keystone references the most strategic part. Holy Spirit had said, "The keystone is being raised in place."

Pentecost is a keystone of the church. So much depended and leaned on it that Jesus commanded His disciples in Acts 1:4, "Don't leave Jerusalem without it. Don't leave until you receive the promise of the Father, because you can't do what you need to do without it. You can't do it in the natural. It will have to come through spiritual means." World evangelism and the discipling of nations depend upon it. The structural beam of the true church leans upon and is supported by a new-era Pentecost. It's locked into position by outpourings of the Spirit and by what occurs at Pentecost.

Holy Spirit and His keystone anointing are central to everything that we do. Signs, wonders, and miracles are dependent upon it. His fresh new Pentecost and outpouring of power is the key to our mission and assignment. It's His presence, His power, His leadership, and His anointing upon which everything else rests. Without it, everything falls apart.

## LORD,

*In these new times of refreshing and outpouring, I posture myself to receive from You. I anchor myself in Your presence, knowing that without it, everything falls apart. Your church needs a fresh infilling of Your Spirit, a new outpouring, the fire of Your presence. Touch us with Your glory that the world may see Your Kingdom established on the earth.*

# THE GREATEST MOVE OF GOD

> **WE DECREE** a mega-outpouring of the Holy Spirit has begun and there is no crisis in the natural realm that can stop this move of God.

I believe we are now moving into a literal new Pentecost, an incredible outpouring of the Holy Spirit. This will be the largest activation in all of church history, and it is due now. Our God's prevailing anointing of favor is going to soak the people of God, the true church, and we are going to see the greatest move of God that has ever been seen on the earth.

All of the streams and all of the moves revealed from Acts 2 until now—everything they individually emphasized, all they taught, all the doctrines they restored, all they meant and established—are now being raised up to lean in place against the keystone, aligned into a new Pentecost. All of them will now function, held together and anointed to succeed by what I can only call a mega outpouring of Holy Spirit.

There is no crisis in the natural realm that can stop it. It will only backfire on hell because the anointing is going to turn things in our favor. It's not that we don't go through crises, because we do. It's not that tough times don't come against us, because they will. It's not that confinement and activities of darkness don't attack us, but we are anointed with favor. The anointing of our God and King, Holy Spirit and His Kingdom, will simply begin to cycle us from barrenness to greater productivity. Greater is He that is in us than He that is in the world (see 1 John 4:4).

206

This is actually the teaching of the New Testament apostles. It is most certainly what the apostle Paul taught the Philippians, writing to them from jail—a place of confinement—which was his punishment for preaching the Gospel of Jesus Christ.

I love this in *The Message* Bible: In Philippians 1:20, Paul states, *"They didn't shut me up; they gave me a pulpit!"*

Paul also wrote in Philippians 1:6, while in confinement, that he was headed for "a flourishing finish." That's a man of faith. This should inspire us and speak to us.

A mega outpouring is beginning to build. The keystone holding it all together is being raised and the true church, the remnant warriors, is headed for a flourishing finish. Your purpose and destiny is headed for a flourishing finish. You are cycling right now into your most productive period. You will now see birthed on this planet what we couldn't birth on our own.

The divisions of angels sent by Holy Spirit are going to help us finish well. They are going to help us break up, break out, break through, passover, and possess a glorious future. We are moving forward from a literal Pentecost into surge after surge of replenishing outpourings from Heaven. The remnant will be soaked with power from on high. Our greatest days are in front of us!

JESUS,

*Your presence has brought us to this place in history—to a mega outpouring of Your Holy Spirit. May Your remnant church rise up and Your warriors be filled afresh to finish the race well. We welcome the assistance of Your angel armies to help us break up, break out, break through, passover and possess the glorious future You have in store!*

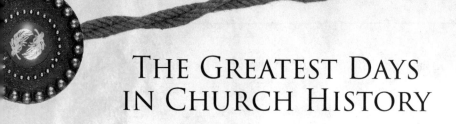

# THE GREATEST DAYS IN CHURCH HISTORY

> **WE DECREE** the bar is raised and
> Holy Spirit is raising the anointing.

New Year's Day, 2020. A new year, new decade, and new era was beginning. I was thinking about our world facing one of its most defining moments. As I pondered world conditions I began to pray, "Holy Spirit, what is King Jesus saying to His church?" He responded with focused clarity that resonated deep in my spirit. It was a challenge to status-quo, passive Christianity. It was bold, decisive, and a call to exercise aggressive faith. "Tell My ekklesia to raise the bar and I'll raise the anointing. Raise the bar and I'll pour out a fresh, new Pentecost greater than Acts 2."

"Raising the bar" is a term that is used in the Olympics. The high jumpers or pole vaulters leap over a bar, and if the bar is cleared it is then raised. This continues until someone clears the highest level and wins the gold medal. This phrase is now used in our times to refer to going to a higher level. I knew Holy Spirit was calling out to the true ekklesia, the reigning church of spiritual governing authority in Jesus' name, to raise the standard, to raise our faith and take genuine New Testament living to another level, to engage in prayer using spiritual weapons of warfare that are not natural—they are mighty through God to the destruction of anti-Christ strongholds.

The call of Heaven couldn't have been clearer. The true church of King Jesus must take its efforts to preach the Gospel of His Kingdom to a new level. "When My heirs raise the bar, I'll raise the anointing and pour out a new Pentecost that will be greater than the outpouring in the Book of Acts."

As I meditated and prayed into this call of Holy Spirit, I began to see amazing purpose and the prophetic destiny He has planned for the true ekklesia of King Jesus. The ekklesia is a spiritual legislating body ruling and reigning with Him in His name. The remnant warriors in Christ's spiritual Kingdom are here to affect the natural kingdoms of the earth, regulating cultures, societies, laws, and discipling nations. I began to see the prophetic destiny of the real ekklesia, functioning in a Holy Spirit-planned purpose for the decades to come.

There has never been anything like it before. All the anointings poured out since the birth of the church, all the vital streams revealing Heaven's truths to man will now flow together and synergize in power. This will all be soaked in a baptism of power from on high. A new Pentecost, with all its precedents, is going to another level.

These plans are now unfolding in times He's prepared. Breakthroughs of healings, miracles, resources, and harvests are on the horizon. Hell will not stop Him as He guides the ekklesia into paths leading into the greatest days in church history.

## HOLY SPIRIT,

*We ready ourselves for what You are about to pour out. We align ourselves with Heaven and ask for understanding of the times that we are in. Thank You that You are now guiding Your ekklesia into the greatest days in church history. I bless Your church today to apprehend every prophetic promise You have stored up for her. We long to operate in Your Holy Spirit-planned purpose!*

# RAISE THE BAR

**WE DECREE** Holy Spirit has the greatest days in church history planned for now.

The New Testament church of Christ's Kingdom will see and live in times Holy Spirit spoke to me about years ago concerning angels saying, "The greatest days in church history are not in your past; they are in your present and your future!" That is His plan and He knows how to do it. Remnant believers in Christ must trust that emphatically and act accordingly. It's time for the radical remnant to follow Holy Spirit to another level.

I believe God does it this way to keep us engaged with Him and from getting ahead of His timing. If He told us everything at once, we might just skip a few things and go straight to the end purpose. It's just human nature. This also allows time to grow our faith. The faith it takes to begin a prophetic journey is usually not enough to finish it. It must keep growing or purpose slows or stagnates. God, in His wisdom, has chosen to grow revelation as we grow our faith. In many ways, an enlightenment journey is also a relationship journey with the Lord, remembering what He has said and pressing into what He is saying.

The prophet Daniel is a great example of this. To understand his times, Daniel went back through the years and read the prophecies concerning the Babylonian captivity. He revisited revelations, visions, dreams, even angel visitations and messages. As he pressed in to seek the Lord with fasting and prayer, the revelation became clear. It's time! It's time for our captivity to end. The 70 years Jeremiah prophesied were ending. They were connecting to their moment.

This understanding enabled Daniel to pray and decree with such bold faith that two of Heaven's strongest angels, Gabriel and Michael, and the divisions of angels they command were sent by Holy Spirit to assist his inter-cession and bring it to pass. The battle lasted 21 days in the atmospheric and astrological heavens against the demon prince of Persia and his army. Heaven's angel armies won. Deliverance came just as God said it would.

Amazingly, the prayer of Daniel and God's people crying out for deliverance was answered by Holy Spirit activating two divisions of angel armies.

This, of course, was done under an old covenant. How much more should this partnership of the Holy Spirit and His angel armies, assisting God's very own heirs, function in a new and better covenant—one Jesus established through His cross. How much more should it operate in Christ's new Kingdom, assisting Christ's very own ekklesia. Certainly, the bar has been raised. Hell has never faced what Holy Spirit has planned for His true Kingdom.

As children of God and joint heirs, we have inalienable Kingdom of Heaven rights. One of those rights is angel assistance. Angels are available to help us maintain our inheritance and, if need be, obtain deliverance and supernatural victories. It's time we operate in this proper Kingdom intention. We must do so at a much higher level if we expect to turn the captivity in nations and live in biblical freedoms. We must raise the bar.

## LORD JESUS,

*I recount Your words today, remembering what You have said and I press in to what You are saying. I believe the greatest days for Your church are in our present and in our future. Thank You that as Your children, we have access to angelic assistance that will bring us into the fullness of Your promises. I ask today for a fresh fire to fall upon Your church as we raise the bar for Your glory!*

# About Tim Sheets

Dr. Tim Sheets is an apostle, pastor of The Oasis Church, the founder of Awakening Now Prayer Network, and author. He travels extensively throughout the nations, carrying his heart and vision for awakening and reformation, the coming generation, and releasing an anointing for signs, wonders, and miracles. He and his wife, Carol, reside in Lebanon, Ohio.

## Contact Information:

www.timsheets.org

Tim Sheets Ministries

6927 Lefferson Road

Middletown, Ohio 45044

carol@timsheets.org

513-424-7150

Facebook: Facebook.com/ApostleTimSheets

Instagram: @TimDSheets